Security
Blankets

ALISON —
I'M TOLD YOU HELPED
GIVE SNOOPY A BIG HEAD
LONG AGO — YOU SHOULD
HAVE TOLD ME о̄
        BEAGLE HUGS —

                DERRICK
                BANG
                5/8/09

Security Blankets

How *Peanuts*® Touched Our Lives

DON FRASER and DERRICK BANG

Andrews McMeel
Publishing, LLC
Kansas City

ISBN-13: 978-0-7407-7105-7
ISBN-10: 0-7407-7105-1

Library of Congress Control Number: 2008042206

09 10 11 12 13 WKT 10 9 8 7 6 5 4 3 2 1

www.andrewsmcmeel.com

Attention: Schools and Businesses

Andrews McMeel books are available at quantity discounts with bulk purchase for educational, business, or sales promotional use. For information, please write to: Special Sales Department, Andrews McMeel Publishing, LLC, 1130 Walnut Street, Kansas City, Missouri 64106.

To Harley Chapman, who in 1956 introduced me to *Peanuts* by giving me a copy of a *Peanuts* reprint book. At the time, we were going through Marine Corps officer training at The Basic School in Quantico, Virginia. Little did Harley know, back then, that he was sending me on a journey that would find me working with Charles "Sparky" Schulz and creating two companies dedicated to *Peanuts* character products. Thank you, Harley, for this gift of a career filled with lifelong friends, and for the satisfaction that comes from bringing "happiness" to so many.

—Don

To Andrea, without whom this book—and its predecessors—would never have existed, because I would never have met and befriended so many wonderful *Peanuts* folks . . . including my coauthor here. Andrea, my eternal thanks for having been so attentive to a "research geek" who greeted you, that first time, laden with five huge notebooks filled with *Peanuts* strips and arcane minutia. (Goodness, what you must have thought!) Bless you for being so kind . . . and so patient!

—Derrick

Foreword

At a point in time when all our relationships seem characterized by the many elements that separate us—religion, politics, environmental concerns, and world affairs—we need to remember and make a point of sharing those things we have in common with family, friends, and even total strangers who live on the other side of the world.

Consider . . . for more than half a century, we've unknowingly bonded—as small towns, as nations, as a world community—through the collective experience of reading a single daily newspaper comic strip: Charles M. Schulz's *Peanuts*.

Popular media—entertainment—has an uncanny gift for helping cultural differences evaporate. The daily cartoonist plays a particularly important role in this vibrant cornucopia: Part humorist, part sage, and part cogent observer of the social condition, a cartoonist is charged with revealing little truths in a modest format that many view as disposable (more's the pity!).

Early cartoonists had no illusions about the permanence of their work; they could not possibly have dreamed of a time, now common in our twenty-first century, when their work might be carefully restored, preserved, and analyzed in gorgeous hardcover books that occupy places of pride on best-seller lists. Back in the day, cartoonists labored solely for the moment, hoping to provoke a smile or—on a particularly good day—a nod of recognition.

Charles Schulz began in a woefully scant seven newspapers when *Peanuts* debuted on October 2, 1950. A staggering 17,897 strips later—now published all over the world, in more than 2,600 newspapers—he finally, reluctantly, put down his pen for the last time. His spirit remained willing, but his body could not oblige.

Although many expected (and feared) that *Peanuts* would fade away altogether, after Schulz's death on February 12, 2000, something entirely different happened. To be sure, some of those thousands of newspapers ran reprint *Peanuts* strips for only a brief period of time, as a gesture of respect, before replacing Schulz's work with something newer and (invariably) far less perceptive or pleasing to the eye. But most newspapers retain their customary dose of *Peanuts* even now, their editors having acknowledged that too many readers still regard the strip as an essential daily experience.

In short, *Peanuts* remains something that *brings people together*. How much else can be said to do that, during these tumultuous times?

Like many of the world's best ideas, the concept for this book began with a question. We'd known each other for years and years, during which we'd independently met hundreds of folks who could point to a significant "*Peanuts* moment" in their lives, just as we had our own vivid Schulzian memories. For a long time, such stories were no more than something to share during social occasions. And then the penny dropped: Just how universal *was* the "*Peanuts* experience"?

The more we thought about this, the more excited we became. Surely the authenticity of intimate personal anecdotes, as filtered through the gentle adventures of Charlie Brown and his friends, would result in a book that people wouldn't be able to put down!

Or so we hoped, anyway. And if you're reading these words, then you must know how we felt.

Putting the concept into motion, however, proved far harder than we'd expected. We were certainly well connected with what could be dubbed the *Peanuts* community, which responded with some of the stories you're about to read. But both of us believed, quite strongly, that the best anecdotes would come from folks with *no* particular involvement with *Peanuts*—either as avid fans or übercollectors—aside from the original comic strip's regular presence in their lives.

But how to *reach* such folks? Ah, that was the supreme challenge. Short of taking out full-page display ads in every large newspaper and popular magazine in the country (in the world?)—something we never could have afforded—how *does* one get the word out? The Internet, ironically, isn't nearly as helpful as one might imagine; the very ease with which information can be spread throughout the Web makes it almost impossible to call attention to one particular appeal for civilian participation.

But we persevered, although the process took more time than we'd expected (and we remain grateful to all our friends and colleagues at Andrews McMeel, for being so patient with us!). Eventually, slowly, *oh* so slowly, the stories began to arrive. First a trickle, then a steady stream. Never a deluge; the word didn't spread quite *that* effectively . . . although we're hoping to have a much easier time with the sequel. (Which brings us to the obligatory plug: If you have a personal *Peanuts*-themed anecdote and would like to share it with the rest of us, flip to page 147 for how-to details.)

Not every submitted story was appropriate, of course. We heard from all sorts of pack rats who boasted of huge collections of *stuff*: not really our mug of root beer. Numerous other folks told us about naming their dogs Snoopy, or their delight at being able to meet Charles Schulz once upon a time, or the humbling experience of a recent trip to the Charles M. Schulz Museum, in Santa Rosa, California. Again, not what we were after.

Describing the perfect submission for *Security Blankets* is a bit like trying to define art: We can't really explain it, but we know it when we see it. But we can say this much: We wanted memories and incidents that literally changed the writers' lives . . . or, at the very least, became a lasting part of their family lore. And while it's true that we were deeply moved by the poignance and understated power of much of what we read, we were just as delighted by stories that derived their impact from simpler, perhaps more amusing events. Some people expressed their relief that Snoopy—in some form—was on hand during a moment of great personal crisis, either during their childhood or adult years. Others acknowledged the degree to which Charlie Brown and his friends had become cultural ambassadors, to ease a transition to the United States from some other homeland. Many compared the passing of Charles Schulz to the loss of a cherished family member. Quite a few shared events that had become family traditions: reading the newspaper comics together, gathering for the annual television airing of *A Charlie Brown Christmas*, baking cookies or trying other recipes from the *Peanuts Cook Book*.

Wanting to emulate Charles Schulz, who jammed a wealth of emotional impact into four small panels, we held out for relatively short stories that could be enjoyed and digested as provocative and enduring appetizers, rather than enormous meals too quickly forgotten. (Bearing that thought in mind, we recommend that you *don't* read this book all at once. Take your time, embracing only a handful of the stories in one sitting, so that the full impact can be derived from each.)

Patience paid off: This book is filled with a blend of heart-warming, droll, and often unexpectedly powerful glimpses into the souls of people who, in "real" life, are total strangers to each other . . . but who, as a result of their shared "*Peanuts* moments," could probably become great friends in a heartbeat.

And we must make something clear: Regardless of the selection process that produced this book, we cherish the time and effort of every single person who wrote. Sharing intimate personal experiences—in some cases, ones of considerable sensitivity—does not come easily to everybody. Those who took a crack at it are to be commended; we salute their bravery. We were also impressed by those who, clearly uncertain of their own writing skills, nonetheless recounted stories that emerged as even more powerful for a use of language that was, perhaps, a little rough around the edges.

We were careful, in turn, not to subject the stories herein to heavy editing. We wanted you, as readers, to be charmed by them in the same way they inspired us.

More than anything else, we were touched by the degree to which many of our contributors insisted upon the profound impact that Charles Schulz and *Peanuts* had made on their lives: an impact that we wish Sparky—as Schulz was known to his friends and family—were around to appreciate.

And yet it's equally clear that all our writers held and shared one more truth: the unswerving belief that (wherever he is)

Sparky *still* derives comfort from the security he has brought to so many thousands upon thousands of people.

We're privileged to share all of the following stories with you, and we cherish this common bond—this shared delight in the adventures that take place in a neighborhood filled with unusually mature children and one wonderfully carefree beagle—that links us so persuasively.

Charlie Brown and Snoopy don't just rule; they're *forever*.

Don Fraser
St. Helena, California

Derrick Bang
Davis, California

December 2008

Acknowledgments

Many books are collaborative efforts, and that's particularly true of this one. Our gratitude is off the charts, our thanks spread among many individuals.

Our biggest gesture of appreciation and respect goes to Charles M. "Sparky" Schulz, without whom . . . well, it doesn't even bear thinking. Suffice it to say that this book is merely one of the humbler efforts that never would have seen the light of day without Sparky's genius to serve as such inspiration.

We must also thank Chris Schillig, our extremely patient editor at Andrews McMeel. (We'll hit our deadlines the next time; we promise!) And, speaking of our publisher, a big shout-out to John McMeel, who—upon hearing about this concept, under purely casual circumstances—encouraged us to produce a prototype and submit it to him. That's the sort of faith that gladdens an author's heart.

Long before a manuscript reaches an official editor, however, it is repeatedly thrust beneath the long-suffering eyes of those trapped by virtue of sharing a home with an author. In our case, then, we owe serious debts of gratitude to Gayna and Dianne, who caught many spelling and punctuation errors before such boo-boos embarrassed us elsewhere.

Jeannie Schulz deserves mention for her encouragement and unfailing kindness.

Which brings us to the true stars of the moment: our contributors, without whom we wouldn't *have* a book. The list is lengthy and alphabetical by necessity, with state—or country—cited, to further demonstrate the degree to which *Peanuts* truly is a universal phenomenon. They're all first among equals, and they all deserve a collective round of applause. Take a deep breath, and recite after us:

Tami Wampach Aker, Minnesota; Merrill Baker, New York; Ellen Kent Beardsley, California; Scott Alan Blanchard, Michigan; Adam Bonner, Michigan; Nancy M. Bosch, California; Ellen M. Brenneman, Indiana; Beth Burkart, California; Mike Burns, New Mexico; Dave Carey, United Kingdom; Diane Carpenter, California; Rachel Crain, California; Robin Dallin-Freyermuth, California; Ann Elizabeth Downard, California; Tracey Dukert, Pennsylvania; Doug Ernst, California; Ed Glazier, California; Jeremy E. Grossman, Indiana; Merideth Hale, Arizona; Gaylord "Hap" Hill, California; Masuhiko Hirobuchi, Japan; Rob Kirby, United Kingdom; Sue Kreft, Oregon; Tomoko Kuroda, Japan; Kathy (Schmit) Letham, British Columbia, Canada; Denny May, Alberta, Canada; Mary McKinney, Arizona; Barbara L. Moler, Virginia; Cindy Cirucci Muders, Pennsylvania; Sallie M. Mugavero, Massachusetts; Nathan Nam, California; Victoria Nguyen-Vu, Connecticut; Shari Noda, California; Christine Nohr, California; Joe Patane (www.joesworld. org), New Jersey; Jay K. Payleitner, Illinois; Andrea Podley, Washington; Jennifer Prystasz, Ontario, Canada; Shano P. Rodgers, California; Heidi Rose, Washington; Sally Bennett Ryen, California; Jason A. Scalese, California; Jennifer Ann Schachner, California; Nicole Schley, New Jersey; David E. Schmidt, Missouri; Karl J. Smith, California; Thomas G. Storey, Arizona; Joyce L. Taub, New York; Joan Wernick, Massachusetts; Kim Hunter Winemiller, North Carolina; and Miranda Wong, Hong Kong.

You're all wonderful, individually and collectively. And when we say we couldn't have done it without you, we really mean it!

Introduction

Storytelling is an ancient art, and yet it's also so modern. My earliest memory of stories came from my Grandma and Grandpa Marvel, and they were truly "*marvel*ous." Every story involved a dog chasing rabbits. You see, we had a beagle named Peanuts. It seems I was destined to one day become the world's most famous beagle.

Since 1979, Snoopy and I have literally been inseparable. Charles "Sparky" Schulz asked me to portray his beagle and perform throughout the world. Snoopy and I have ridden an Olympic bobsled, directed the Mormon Tabernacle Choir, performed in the Super Bowl halftime show, and even floated in zero gravity, just like the astronauts.

During the thousands of hugs that Snoopy and I have shared with you all, I've loved hearing the stories that people tell him: the little girls who whisper loudly, as they lift Snoopy's velvet ear, "I want to tell you a secret"; or the teenage boys who usually begin their tales with "Yo, Snoop! 'Sup?" Then there's always some adult who says, "Have you heard the one about the beagle who walked into the root beer bar . . . ?"

Stories can be told in many forms. Because Snoopy doesn't talk, I must communicate warmth, laughter, and fear through fuzzy mime. Verbal stories change in the telling and require good listening and reporting skills. The written story best captures the feelings, and records them for all time.

Charles Schulz has left us brilliant characters in words and pictures, and his work has inspired all of us to see the stories in our own lives. This book is a gift to those of us who knew Sparky personally. It allows us to experience the unique intersection of

hearts and a comic strip, or a stuffed animal or toy. I personally thank each and every person who has contributed to this book. In so doing, you have given us the insight into how Sparky's characters always will be remembered as parts of ourselves.

Judy Sladky
(A close personal friend of Snoopy's)
New Jersey, December 2008

Security
Blankets

Nicole Schley

Snoopy and the *Peanuts* crew have always been a part of my life, but not much will ever compare to the feeling I had as a child, when I received my first plush Snoopy.

I was seven years old, and Christmas was approaching quickly. My friends and I discussed at great length what we hoped Santa would bring us on that glorious, magical day. Instead of visions of sugarplums dancing in our heads, we had visions of toys underneath our Christmas trees.

This was the year when rumors started to spread that Santa Claus might not exist. Kids were saying that their older siblings had told them that their parents *really* bought the gifts. Questions arose about flying reindeer, and how a fat man in a big red suit could get down all those chimneys (especially when I didn't even have one).

I set out to prove the existence of Santa.

My mom and I had been shopping in the mall, and I noticed a plush Snoopy in one of the stores. He was magnificent. He looked so soft: the perfect size to cuddle and hold. That same day, I went to see the mall Santa for my annual visit. I couldn't wait to tell him about the plush Snoopy. Then I sat on his lap and discussed my Wish List, which included everything *except* Snoopy. I was devastated when I walked away and realized that I had forgotten to tell my only connection to the North Pole about what I really wanted.

Then I realized that I could use this to my advantage: This could prove to me—and the rest of the world—whether Santa Claus truly existed. In my seven-year-old mind, I devised a theory: If Santa actually did exist, he'd already know that I wanted this plush Snoopy. So I took a risk and did not include the plush Snoopy on my mailed Christmas list, when it was sent to Santa that year.

I remember waking up that Christmas morning, walking out to the living room, and with great amazement admiring the Christmas tree, with all those gifts underneath. I set out on a mission, unwrapping gift after gift. But the pile was diminishing, and then I came across one of the last possible boxes that might be large enough for my plush friend. I slowly unwrapped it and noticed two long black ears, two eyeballs . . . and, yes, that big beagle nose! My plush Snoopy was staring back at me, and I was utterly amazed. I stood, wide eyed, and quickly took him out of his wrapping. I hugged him and jumped up and down, shouting,

"Now I *know* that Santa exists, because I wanted Snoopy so bad and didn't tell anyone!"

Decades have passed since I was united with my favorite plush beagle. His pajamas are faded, and his originally large nose and white fluffy head are squished. But since that Christmas Day twenty-six years ago, we've never been apart. He went to college with me, traveled across the country on softball tournaments—he stayed in my bag, to provide me with security while being away from home—and even went into the operating room when I had surgery a few years ago. (The doctor put scrubs on Snoopy, too!)

He has been my best friend and confidant. Happiness truly is—and will always be—my first plush Snoopy.

Rachel Crain

A friend once told me that you can judge people by asking which *Peanuts* character they most identify with. He told me their answer will give all you need to know about who they really are.

I told him that I identify with Sally, because of her unrequited and constant love for Linus. The little hearts that float, sparkle, and explode all around her head every time Linus is nearby remind me of how I felt every time my crush—my "Linus"—came around.

I've always gotten a kick out of how Linus appears to be bothered by Sally's advances. But we know, deep down, that if Sally ever turned her affections away, he'd feel alone and wish that she and her floating hearts would reappear, to shower him with love.

We caught a glimpse of this in TV's *It's the Great Pumpkin, Charlie Brown*, when Sally, exasperated by Linus's preoccupation with the Great Pumpkin, left him all alone and friendless in the pumpkin patch, without any treats, to cry over another wasted Halloween spent waiting for the hero who'd never appear.

I like to imagine, in the unwritten stories of the *Peanuts* gang as grown-ups, that Linus would finally understand that the fulfillment he sought in the Great Pumpkin was—all the time—right in front of him, in Sally's very real love. I like to believe this is how it would have turned out for them, because this is how it turned out for me, a real-life Sally, and Joshua, my real-life Linus.

Joshua and I knew each other for six years before he returned my feelings. He tells me now that he spent a lot of time looking for love, thinking it was mysterious and illusive, when everything he was seeking was right in front of him, with me.

Romantic?

Yes, but the waiting was the hardest part!

Because of her constant suffering over Linus, Sally is my kindred spirit. But referring to Joshua as my "Linus" always was something of a joke: a convenient comparison, since I related to Sally so deeply.

And yet, after Joshua and I were married, Linus (unlike the Great Pumpkin) really did show up. My "Sweet Babboo" even came with a security blanket. (He hogs the covers at night.) And the parallels don't end there.

Like Sally, I love to write. She makes herself busy with letters and homework, the same way I spend time with church newsletter assignments and long e-mails to friends. Like Linus, Joshua doesn't see the world in black and white; you can also count on a philosophical argument over whether the variations in between should be labeled as gray.

Like Sally, I have a blockhead older brother—times two—and a family dog who is smarter than all of us.

When I look at all the people in my life, I see the kids from the *Peanuts* gang everywhere. I see another classically unrequited love story between Lucy and Schroeder, in my bossy older sister, Nichol, and her husband, Andy, the tortured artist. I see Woodstock's fragility and carefree youth in my nieces Kealie and Collette. And I recognize the walking disaster that is Pigpen in a person who—for the sake of protection—shall remain nameless.

Maybe my friend was right: All we need to know about a person can be determined by learning which *Peanuts* character strikes a chord.

Fortunately for me, Charles Schulz's world—with all its wit and wisdom—is filled with exactly the kind of characters I want to know, and love, and learn from.

And maybe even live as . . . if only in the funny pages.

Karl J. Smith

In 1972, when I was writing my first textbook, I wanted to include some *Peanuts* cartoons. At that time, such items never appeared in college math textbooks, so I scheduled a meeting with Charles M. Schulz at his office. I remember the meeting clearly: Mr. Schulz was unassuming, asked me about my project, and then assigned me to one of his staff for the help I needed.

My book was published in 1973. Shortly after I received the first copies, I autographed one, thanked Mr. Schulz for his help, and delivered the book to his office. He thanked me and said that he was asked by many for his help, but it was rare that someone thanked him after they no longer wanted something from him.

Several years passed. Then, on January 13, 1979, when I was reading the *Santa Rosa Press Democrat* in order to get my daily dose of good cheer, I looked at *Peanuts*. To my surprise, Mr. Schulz had used a problem from my book.

I shouted out to my wife: "That's my problem!"

My next thought was "Wait! I obtained permission to use his work in my book; did he get permission to use my work in his cartoon?" I took a closer look, and, sure enough, my problem was enclosed in quotation marks.

But that wasn't all! The next day, I received a mailing tube; when I looked inside, I found something that remains one of my most treasured possessions: the original hand-drawn cartoon. At the top, Mr. Schulz had written, "To Karl, with friendship and appreciation. Charles M. Schulz."

A few weeks later, a letter from his secretary arrived at my home, also expressing Mr. Schulz's appreciation. The letter said, in part, "We've had a lot of fun with fans writing to find the solution, and one seventh grader from San Jose says her algebra teacher can't do the problem, and he'll give her extra credit if she can come up with the answer."

That book has gone through eleven editions, and the cartoon has appeared in every edition since the third, published in 1980. About ten years ago, I was refused permission to use it and the others by United Feature Syndicate, the copyright holder, because they had a "rule" about not giving permission to use "old" *Peanuts* comic strips. Once again, I turned to Mr. Schulz, with my request to include this comic strip; he complied by writing a letter to his syndicate to give me permission to print it (as long as I complied with all usual payments). I believe he understood the power of *Peanuts* to reach students who otherwise might not look at a math textbook.

I've related this story and shown the comic strip every year in my classes at Santa Rosa Junior College, and during presentations at various mathematics conferences. Almost every time, someone comes up and relates his or her own *Peanuts* story, or asks a question like "Did you *really* meet Charles Schulz?"

Yes, Mr. Schulz and *Peanuts* have been a part of my books and my teaching for more than thirty years. Thank you, Charlie Brown!

Dave Carey

I am from Liverpool, England, and my first encounter with *Peanuts* took place in the early 1970s, when I would have been seven or eight years old.

My beloved older sister, ten years my senior and the kindest, gentlest girl in the world, had just come out of a bad relationship. She decided she had had enough of Liverpool and would join the British army, to get as far away from the place as possible. The thought of her leaving was devastating; I genuinely believed I might never see her again and spent the evening before her departure crying at the foot of the stairs. The next morning, before I was even awake, she was gone.

For a few weeks, there was nothing; not a word was heard from her, and my conviction that she had forgotten all about us deepened. Then, one afternoon, I came home from school and found my parents behaving strangely. Through all their nods and winks, it was clear that something was up. I couldn't imagine what it could be, until my sister walked out of the kitchen. She had told my parents she was coming home for the weekend, but that they shouldn't tell me, so it would be a surprise.

She had brought a little present for me: two Coronet books of *Peanuts* reprints, called *Slide, Charlie Brown! Slide!* and *All This and Snoopy, Too*. I had never heard of Charlie Brown or Snoopy, but I started reading the books out of curiosity and instantly fell in love with the characters therein. The sequence where Charlie Brown fails to "steal home"—an expression that meant little to me at the time, ignorant as I was of American baseball—and lies on the ground making cries of anguish . . . I still can remember how poignant and dramatic I found that.

That started a tradition. Every time my sister came home for a visit—usually as a delightful surprise—she'd always bring one or two Coronet *Peanuts* books for me. The joy I found in those books became a part of the joy I found in anticipating her next visit. Gradually, my little pile of *Peanuts* books grew higher and higher, and I would take huge pleasure in rereading the books. They spoke to me of my sister. When I was missing her particularly strongly, I would open (for example) *You're a Brave Man, Charlie Brown* and lose myself in the rich warmth and humour of the books. They always brought me closer to her.

My sister is dead now. She died at the age of forty-three, in particularly upsetting circumstances. The Coronet books will always be a memento to her; although I plan to collect all the Fantagraphics books, I'll never relinquish the Coronets. I owe a huge debt to Charles Schulz. The warm, contemplative, compassionate world that I found in his books enabled me to lose myself at times, when my own world seemed too lonely and hard to bear: when the one person who made it bearable was such an awful long way away.

There will simply never be anything like those stories.

Tami Wampach Aker

When I was twelve, my Dad bought me a sweatshirt with a character on it that I'd never seen before. The caption on the sweatshirt was *Curse you, Red Baron!* and it had a beagle dressed as a World War I Flying Ace, sitting on a bullet-ridden doghouse. This was my introduction to Snoopy, and the start of a lifelong passion. After the sweatshirt came a Snoopy pocket doll, and then my dreams came true when I received my first Snoopy plush. I still have all my first collector items, with the plush displayed very prominently in his blue Snoopy-footed sleeper. After my Mom passed away, I looked for my prized sweatshirt for many years and feared that I'd never see it again, but she had carefully packed it away in our attic. She knew I'd look for it again. I cried when I found it.

My passion for Snoopy continued to grow, and my original plush Snoopy accompanied me to boarding school and then college. Looking back, it was funny: The older I got, the more I didn't seem to care what people thought about my Snoopy passion, or if they thought me immature because of it.

Snoopy really started to become more important to me as I progressed further in my career. I've been a police officer for twenty-seven years, and there hasn't been much I haven't seen or done throughout this career. I did my time as a street cop in our city's worst neighborhoods. I was an administrator. It didn't take me too long, as a big-city cop, to realize how important it was to have something in my personal life that grounded me, no matter what went on in my professional life.

Snoopy was that stabilizer for me: my consistent inward escape to happiness. Snoopy was the one thing that could always make me smile. When I was a sergeant, I was called Sergeant Snoopy. Now that I'm a lieutenant and commander of the Minneapolis Police Department's crime lab, I have a plush Snoopy dressed as Sherlock Holmes—holding a real magnifying glass—sitting on my desk. He's the unit mascot. I get teased about having been able to get license plates that say SNOOPY, because I had an "in" as a cop. (Maybe it helped just a little!)

My husband claims that I was a closet collector before we got married, and he teases me about not letting on how bad my problem was until "it was too late." Shortly before my Dad passed away, I reminded him about the time when he told me in high school that I would "outgrow" Snoopy; he laughed, realizing he couldn't have been more wrong about anything. I hope Sparky knew what a great influence he had on so many people, and that through him and Snoopy, some of us *did* find our true meaning of happiness.

Miranda Wong

This is a story of love at first sight, between a Hong Kong Chinese girl named Miranda and Snoopy.

On September 3, 1977, the first day of a new school year, I saw a cute little dog on my classmate's pencil case. The doggy was standing on his right leg, with his body slightly tilted to the right. His head was in the shape of a peanut. He didn't have a mouth, yet his eyes seemed to be talking. Beneath his feet was the word *Snoopy*. He was irresistibly charming, and I really liked him.

In the 1970s, *Peanuts* products were very rare in Hong Kong. Most were imported and very expensive. Even though I could not afford any, I still enjoyed going to department stores once in a while just to appreciate the *Peanuts* items, hoping that one day I might own a few Snoopy things.

Miranda, age fifteen

Months later, I found a free-of-charge way to keep in touch with Snoopy . . . something even better than window-shopping! Oh, why hadn't anyone told me that *Peanuts* comic strips were in the news-papers? After that, I became a frequent visitor to the public library. In the beginning, I only had half the fun. Owing to my English standards and limited knowledge of sports and American culture, I couldn't understand all the strips. But I still loved to see them.

Snoopy is my favorite character, and not only because he was the first character I knew. The greater reason is that we have something in common: a connection that is hard to explain in words. When I was a kid, I loved to lean on the windowsill, watching the outside world, and letting my imagination take me away. I used to think about hover-ing between planets, or traveling around the world in a soap bubble. What if, one day, I became a detective, a giraffe, or a cloud? What if there were ten identical copies of me? When I saw Snoopy's different personas, I just laughed out loud. It was an incredibly warm feeling to find some dog out there sharing the same experiences!

I liked the other characters, too, as I could see so much of myself in them. They helped me understand more about myself and the peo-ple around me. I began to appreciate the wittiness of Charles Schulz. How could one single person come up with so many inspiring ideas, day after day? It was just amazing.

The *Peanuts* experience opened up a brand-new world for me. I met some great artists and sculptors. I visited Santa Rosa and Min-neapolis, listened to jazz, and learned about things that I otherwise might have been less interested in. After joining the Peanuts Collec-tor Club, I made friends with some of the nicest people I've ever met. They taught me a lot of things, including the joy of sharing. I really have to thank God for letting me find Snoopy. Life without Sparky and Snoopy would never be quite the same.

A friend once asked if I'd still love Snoopy at the age of eighty. My answer:

"Definitely! My love for Snoopy is everlasting. If you take a look at my cells under a microscope, you'll probably find that each and every one of them is in the shape of Snoopy's head!"

Merideth Hale

I was an avid third-grade reader of both books and the newspaper when *Peanuts* first was syndicated in the *Minneapolis Star* in the 1950s. The *Peanuts* characters have been part of my daily life since then. After graduating from college, I taught fourth grade and special learning disabilities. *Peanuts* calendars and seasonal paper products were always part of my classroom decor. Later, as clothing and jewelry appeared on the market, I wore those frequently and carried a Snoopy lunch box. Snoopy stickers went onto student papers. All students quickly recognized that I liked Snoopy, Woodstock, and the other characters.

I retired in 1994, after teaching for thirty years, and moved to Arizona and began to volunteer once a week in a friend's (Mary Kuopus's) second-grade classroom in Scottsdale. Each year, as she introduces me to her students, she tells them that I enjoy and collect the *Peanuts* characters. The children readily notice this each time I come into the room: My earrings, my water bottle, my purse, and my sweaters or sweatshirts always have some *Peanuts* character, usually Snoopy or Woodstock. Some students also proudly wear *Peanuts*-character T-shirts or sweatshirts on the days I am expected.

In the classroom, I do whatever Mrs. Kuopus needs done: help children write journals or letters, complete assignments, correct papers, listen to them read, read to them, etc. Each spring, she has a bird unit. Because I love birds, I help by teaching the children birding vocabulary, how to identify birds, how to use a field guide, and the enjoyment of birding.

We work on bird projects with small groups for a period of several months. Small groups help me know the children, and they get needed individual attention. One seven-year-old boy, Chance, sat near another student I was frequently asked to help, either to get started or to keep at an assignment. Chance would ask for help when he needed it but basically completed his work without much additional assistance. He was the oldest of five children and the only boy. Mrs. Kuopus said his basic interest was "life." He loved doing almost

I hope you have a very Snoopyrifick birthday.

Your friend,

Chance

anything but particularly sports. Chance often joined our bird-watching groups at recess (this was voluntary) as we wandered around the school grounds looking for birds and observing their behavior.

Children in this classroom spend part of each day writing, either in a daily journal or in their educational logs. Letters are sometimes written for specific reasons. Chance wrote this particular letter to me for two reasons: It was my birthday and also my last day of that school year, 2005–6. It read, in part:

5-18-06

Dear Mrs. Hale,

Thank you for volunteering every Thursday Mrs. Hale. Happy birthday Mrs. Hale. Thank you so much for teaching us all about bird sounds, bird riddles, birds habitats, and teaching us how to use a bird guide.

Thank you for teaching us how to go birding. It is not fun to go birding, it is Super fun to go birding!

Mrs. Hale, I hope you have a great birthday.

I hope you have a very Snoopyrifick birthday.

Your friend,
Chance

I had never used the word *Snoopyrifick* and, to my knowledge, neither had his teacher. He had asked his teacher for help with several of the words, but not *Snoopyrifick*. This was a delightful surprise to her, as well.

I not only had a Snoopyrifick birthday, but I've certainly had many Snoopyrifick experiences, both in the classroom during my many years of teaching and volunteering and in my daily life . . . all because of the wonderful characters created by Charles M. Schulz.

Nancy M. Bosch

Three nights a week, five hours each time: That was the routine—as I remember it—of my mom's life as a dialysis patient. My dad was often unsure of what to do with two girls on those long nights, but he couldn't go wrong with shopping. My sister, like a targeted missile, headed for the teen clothing department; I, with outstretched arms, went to the pyramid of Snoopys. I was perfectly content to sit at the base of the display, week after week. My dad must have observed this strange behavior, because one day he said, "Do you want one?"

Shocked by the question, I uttered, "Uh-huh."

"Pick one, then."

I hadn't prepared for this moment; I never thought I'd have one of my own. I felt like a contestant on *The Price Is Right*, with people yelling: "The one on the right . . . higher . . . lower!" I panicked, took a deep breath, and rejoiced at the task before me. I sorted through many Snoopys, examining each one. "This one's eye is crooked." "His head is turned." "His tail is flat." "This one is dirty."

Nestled among his brothers, there he was: my Snoopy!

When my family went to sleep, Snoopy was there when I waited up for my mom to get home from dialysis at ten o'clock. He provided a warm, affirming smile. I spent hours looking at his features, from his threaded black eyes down to his stitched toes. I created "hairdos" with his ears (Indian Snoopy), dressed him in a checkered shirt and pair of blue jeans for everyday wear, and on special occasions added a cowboy vest. Every year, we watched *A Charlie Brown Christmas* and *It's the Great Pumpkin, Charlie Brown* together.

Snoopy was also there on the final night I waited up to say goodnight to my mom. Snoopy became my "invisible" friend, my conscience and inner voice in uncertain times. I never hesitated to consult him telepathically when I needed his advice. (Not many people know he's telepathic.) He continued to watch over all the other animals, bringing security and hugs especially to me.

After my mother's death, I grew up with several new mothers, lived in numerous houses, and lost many memories and trinkets along the way. Snoopy had been given to me when I was a lonely child during my mother's illness, and he grew up with me as a child without a mother. Although the memories have withered, the smells faded, and the once familiar touch and voices are long gone, Snoopy is what remains of my past that offers comfort and familiarity. Today, if someone says they

like Snoopy, I smile and instantly have memories of talking to, dressing, and carrying Snoopy. I *could* talk about his cute face, big nose, and funny laugh. However, the adult in me simply nods in agreement.

I'm thirty-three years old, and I love Snoopy. I love him for providing love, friendship, and comfort to a young child. He's the token of wholeness and security left from my youth. I'm thankful to have had him in my life.

Barbara L. Moler

I've loved Snoopy since I was a very young child, when my parents would take my brother and me to visit our grandparents on weekends. We would stay with them once or twice a month, so Mom and Dad could go out on Saturday nights.

I loved those weekends, spending time with my grandparents. On Sunday mornings, my Granddad would take us to Sunday school and church. The first few years, I was so young that I couldn't read. I remember looking forward to coming home from Sunday school: While my grandmother fixed lunch, Granddad would pull the Sunday funnies out of the newspaper. (That's what they called them in the 1950s.)

Peanuts became my favorite cartoon strip. After I got older, I found out it was Granddad's favorite, as well. I would crawl onto his lap to listen to him read them aloud while I looked at the cartoons. This would take a very long time, as my grandfather would start reading the comic to me and then laugh so hard, or get so tickled about one of Charles Schulz's sketches, that lunch was ready by the time we finished the *Peanuts* strip. And back then, Sunday lunch after church wasn't just a sandwich and chips, but fried chicken, mashed potatoes with gravy, and two vegetables . . . plus dessert. So you can imagine how long it took to read that Sunday *Peanuts* strip!

When I learned how to read, we reversed the roles: I read to Granddad while sitting on his lap, both of us still laughing and discussing the cartoons.

I was born in February 1950 and have grown up reading (or hearing) the *Peanuts* comic strip all my life. I now get my daily dose of early *Peanuts* strips—and memories of my grandfather—by reading from the books in *The Complete Peanuts* series. I also read the daily newspaper-strip reprint and the daily desk calendar. No day goes by that I don't get my dose of *Peanuts* in some form.

I only had a few Snoopy items by the time I was twenty-four. I married my husband, Gary, in June 1974; shortly thereafter, he began working for a men's clothing store. He became friends with two coworkers,

Barbara, age five, and her grandfather

Denny and Wayne. Gary would invite one or the other home for dinner, as they all worked in the evening, and both men lived out of town.

One evening, when both Denny and Wayne came for dinner, I was reading a *Peanuts* book when they arrived. They asked about this; my husband told them about my grandfather, and how I began to love Snoopy. The next time Gary brought the guys home for dinner, they arrived with a large bag filled with every *Peanuts* ornament they could find in the local mall, as a thank-you gift for all the dinners I had made for them.

Today, I have thirty-two years' worth of Snoopy and the *Peanuts* gang ornaments on my Christmas tree. My home is decorated with various animated Snoopy figures and every holiday item imaginable.

Thank you, Granddad, for sharing Snoopy with me when I was so young.

I love you!

Masuhiko Hirobuchi

It was early summer in 1965. A Japanese television network assigned me as a correspondent to New York City, where I had a happy encounter with Snoopy and his friends. As I had felt the need to polish up my English, to be more communicative with American people, I was looking for someone who would teach me "refined English." I visited the Midtown International Center, where a young lady tutor recommended that I read *The Wonderful World of Peanuts*. The book was full of charming conversations among the magnificent kids. They were really fascinating, and I could feel that my English was dramatically improving. Later, *The Peanuts Treasury*, a thick compilation of masterpieces, impressed me even more. While enjoying the verbal expressions, I appreciated the profound insight into the life of Charles Schulz.

Peanuts also provided us foreigners with precious information about American life, especially about people's mentality and emotions. I could learn many things, such as a son's love and respect for his father, through Charlie Brown's behavior.

In 1969, NASA named the Apollo 10 lunar module *Snoopy*, and its command module *Charlie Brown*. At that time, both the dog and the boy were not yet introduced to the Japanese market. I had a terrible time explaining to the audience what Snoopy and Charlie Brown were all about, and why NASA had adopted these nicknames. Can you imagine how difficult it was to tell about things that people had never seen? In addition to that, I had to explain the mental or spiritual "meaning" of Snoopy and Charlie Brown. Apparently, NASA used these names because they represented the hearts and minds of grassroots Americans. But how could a television correspondent explain the hidden meaning of these characters in very short words?

Impossible!

Almost twenty-five years later, Snoopy goods flooded the Japanese market, but people still didn't seem to understand the real "meaning" of Snoopy. They simply loved a visible or "touchable" Snoopy. His mental or spiritual facet was not known. There was a huge perception gap about Snoopy between our two nations. Someone had to narrow that gap. I thought it was my role to do the job, so I started writing *Snoopy tachino America* [*A Journalist's View of America Through Peanuts*]. The book was published by Shinchosha in 1993. In this book, I tried to portray something internal to American life: Why do

Americans like Charlie Brown so much? Why does Lucy have a psychiatric booth? Why does Snoopy dress as an attorney? And so on.

The publication was a fantastic success. It went into fifteen printings during nine years. Japanese people began to realize something substantial about *Peanuts*, but the majority of them still didn't know the "meaning" of Snoopy.

In September 2006, my fourth book about *Peanuts—Words and Philosophy May Change Your Life, Snoopy*—was published by Kairyusha.

My effort to narrow the perception gap on Snoopy across the Pacific Ocean still goes on!

Diane Carpenter

My daughter, Soraya Esmaili, was turning five; for her birthday, she requested that we go ice-skating. (She's twenty-eight years old now, so this story took place quite some time ago.) We had a wonderful time that sunny May day, skating and falling down and laughing. We ran into some friends who we hadn't seen in a couple of years, so the day became even more special.

After skating, Soraya and I headed to Santa Rosa's Warm Puppy Café for a birthday treat, since her actual birthday party was to be held the following day with friends and family. We also needed to rest our bruised bones before continuing the rest of our day.

Soraya wanted a chocolate ice cream cone, since this was a treat usually not offered at home. While we were sitting at our table in the filled café, Mr. Schulz came in and began greeting the many customers, strolling from table to table. We happened to have an extra chair at our table, and he asked if he could join us for a minute. While talking to us, he learned it was Soraya's birthday, so he took a napkin and autographed it for her. As he was leaving to move on to the next table, Soraya grabbed the napkin and used it to wipe the melting chocolate ice cream off her chin.

Being a good little girl, she hopped off her chair and threw the crumpled, dirty, autographed napkin into the trash can and came back to the table.

Now that Soraya is a married woman, she still enjoys hearing this story time and time again. And she asks why I didn't stop her.

She was just too quick!

Joyce L. Taub

I always loved the *Peanuts* comic strip, but I *truly* fell in love with the characters when my brother—older by five years—went off to college.

Before that, he spent plenty of time during our growing years taking advantage of the little sister who worshipped him. I would do anything for him, despite getting no show of gratitude. But when my brother went off to college, I think he came to realize that I had some value, and he actually missed me. During his first visit back home, that October, he gave me—either as a show of love or a truce—a *Peanuts* calendar he had purchased at the university bookstore. If it had been a piece of jewelry, I wouldn't have cherished it more. It was actually called a date book, and, oh, how I wished I could have been asked out on a "date," so I could write an appropriate entry!

The date book was spiral bound, and I kept it propped up against the wall behind my desk. It had great big boxes for each date, and *Peanuts* strips at the bottom of each month, as well as one giant *Peanuts* "joke" on the month's flip side. But those weren't really jokes; they were life lessons. I was a teenager, thinking, "Poor Charlie Brown" (and poor me, too). Some days, I felt just like him: "I only dread one day at a time." Other days, I felt like Lucy: "Can I help it if I was born with crabby genes?" Because of Schroeder's love of Beethoven, one of the dates highlighted was Beethoven's birthday, on December 16.

Years passed; I got married. Imagine our delight when our first son was born on December 16, 1970. Each year, that date was a brightly colored square on the *Peanuts* calendar.

In the early 1990s, I shared my love of the *Peanuts* date book with a friend; each year, we would alternate who would buy two copies, and give one to the other of us. When in 1997 neither of us could find a 1998 date book—neither in New York nor in Florida—we made calls, wrote letters, and grimly had to accept the fact that it no longer was being published. *Good grief!*

The *Peanuts* characters were my constant daily companions for thirty-seven years. In my date books, I could look back to see where I went and with whom, what I wore, what movies we saw, when I had my hair cut. I could look ahead and see how many appointments I had in one day, when my papers were due, and whose birthday was coming (buy a *Peanuts* card). All the while, I was learning that my thoughts, trials, and stresses were not unusual, because they were validated by the *Peanuts* gang and Charles Schulz. THE DOCTOR IS IN—it was a comfort to think I could get psychiatric help with the turn of a page!

In my own home, I still have every calendar from the year I was married (1968) through 1997. I'm sure I can find the earlier ones in my old room, in my parents' home. And the best thing of all? My brother never knew he started something until I spoke of his *Peanuts* gift to me, during a speech I made on his sixtieth birthday. He was stunned that I had valued it so . . . and he doesn't "stun" easily. Like Lucy, he knows *everything!*

I've learned that confidence is a good thing.

And I will never forget Beethoven's birthday.

Kathy (Schmit) Letham

Snoopy graduated from the University of Wisconsin at Superior in 1971; was in the delivery room for the birth of two baby girls; taught music and dance at an elementary school in Canada for twenty-six years; has traveled all over the world; and has run sixteen Bloomsday Races in Spokane, Washington.

And he still smiles.

Snoopy experienced all these milestones right by my side.

Ever since I was a little girl growing up in the tiny town of Tomahawk, Wisconsin, in the 1950s and '60s, I've loved Snoopy and empathized with Charles Schulz's *Peanuts* characters.

In 1969, I received a pair of Snoopy earrings as a gift. He has been with me ever since, throughout my lifetime.

When I soloed for the first time in my dad's airplane, Snoopy was in awe of the vastness and wonder of the skies.

When I fell in love, married a hockey player, and moved two thousand miles from my hometown to start a new life in Terrace, British Columbia, Canada, Snoopy was there.

I've always been honored to wear these earrings, and Snoopy has witnessed many amazing happenings in my life, large and small: performances in concerts, dance recitals, and music festivals; cheering at hockey tournaments; watching Fourth of July parades; taking in a Green Bay Packers game at Lambeau Field; hiking and skiing in the mountains of British Columbia; swimming across lakes in Canada and the United States; enjoying camping and fishing trips; playing in badminton tournaments; cycling the Oregon coast; and celebrating at birthday parties and holiday festivities.

Snoopy has been present for monumental events, too: births, graduations, weddings, retirement parties (for my husband and me), and even funerals.

Anyone who knows me also knows how special and important Snoopy is to me. He has always whispered in my ear: "Enjoy life to the fullest!"

Over the past thirty-seven years, every time I've worn those special earrings, Snoopy has been right there at my side, through all the highs and lows: sharing all those memorable moments with me; celebrating with tears of joy at happy times with family and friends; and sharing tears of sorrow at overwhelming challenges and the loss of loved ones.

And when my precious grandchildren ask why I always wear these earrings, I'll tell them, "Perhaps Snoopy is so special to me because he was born right around the same time I was. He's a charming dog who is my best buddy—my most faithful companion—and I know I can count on him. We all need a lifelong friend like Snoopy."

Don't we?

Ann Elizabeth Downard

I've been a Snoopy fan for as long as I remember. When I was about ten years old, my best friend and I made an agreement that I'd get her a plush rabbit for Christmas if she got me a plush Snoopy. The pact was fulfilled, and I had my first Snoopy. He sat up with a collar and red dog tag. I slept with him until he needed to be retired. He was followed by many others.

I've suffered from disabilities and disorders since I was an infant. To better cope with the horrific treatment I received from my parents, foster parents, and then adoptive parents, I "created" other people to stay alive.

I related to Snoopy because he has so many personalities: He made me smile, and he took me away from the present moment. Having a Snoopy plush of my own meant everything to me. He hugged me, listened to me, and was my best friend. I could always count on him to be there for me.

When one of my Snoopys gets worn out, I retire him to a special box. I've never thrown one away. I have them in all different sizes, made of all different materials. He sleeps with me and goes everywhere with me. We have a dog that loves doggy stuffed animals, but she knew from the beginning not to touch my Snoopy. I don't know *how* she knows, but I can sleep soundly without worrying that she'll chew Snoopy to bits.

One funny story took place when the neck of one Snoopy started to come apart. My husband took him to a cleaning and alterations business to see if they could fix him. The next day, my husband returned to pick Snoopy up and found that he had a green ribbon around his neck with a piece of candy tied to it. When my husband tried to pay for the repair, the store personnel said that Snoopy had been such a good boy that they were happy to do the job and gave him back to my husband for free! They'd had to take the stuffing out in order to clean him, then stuffed him back up and stitched the neck, and he was good to go.

Another problem I sometimes have is that a plush Snoopy's eyebrows and nose will fall apart. I've been able to fix his eyebrows, but once his nose starts to fall apart, it's like loose spaghetti. One time, one of my neighbors took apart a knit black glove and made a pom-pom real tight and then sewed it onto Snoopy. No one could tell that it was a new nose. I was truly grateful.

As you've probably guessed, I'm an easy person to shop for. I get a little obsessed, to say the least, and so do some of my friends. One friend in particular likes to tease me about my love of Snoopy. One evening, he and his wife were at our house for dinner. When I was cleaning up and had my back turned; my friend put my Snoopy in the freezer. As time went by, while we watched TV, he asked if we had any ice cream. When I opened the freezer door, I found Snoopy. He was cold, but he still had that famous smile on his face.

Snoopy and I will always be best friends. He has helped me in so many ways. He doesn't take life too seriously, and he always has a plan and enjoys his many experiences.

If only he could get back at the darn cat next door and catch the Red Baron.

Charles M. Schulz touched my life by creating a friend forever.

Nathan Nam

The rain fell softly on my head as I approached the marker. I saw mementos left behind by previous visitors to the site: a button, a candle, a letter scrawled on notebook paper weighed down by a rock.

Should I leave something, too?

This visit to the Pleasant Hills Cemetery in Sebastopol was the culmination of a lifetime of appreciation for a man I'd never met, yet to whom I felt closer than members of my own family.

Charles Schulz led an extraordinary life. In some odd way, I feel I was a part of it.

I arrived in America at age six, not knowing a word of English. Some

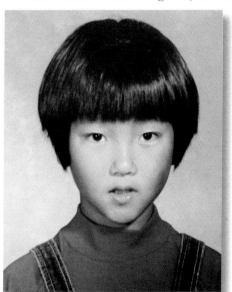

Nathan, age seven

people have fond memories of their childhood. I do not. To me, America was a nightmare of bigotry and racial slurs everywhere I went. Total strangers would make "ching-chong" noises or pull their eyes to look slanted as I walked by. The never-ending barrage of racist assaults, from both children and adults, made every day a living hell. I felt miserable and alone.

So, I escaped into books, *Peanuts* books in particular. I had read other comics before, but for some reason *Peanuts* always stuck with me . . . because there was something very peculiar about it.

Peanuts featured a kid named Charlie Brown, and nobody liked him.

In every single book I read, Charlie Brown was belittled and abused by everyone. I realized something: Someone out there in the world was just as lonely as I was.

And I didn't feel so alone anymore.

For once, I wasn't the only weirdo with a freakishly large head that everyone made fun of. I wasn't the only loser who failed at every sport he ever played. I wasn't the only one who was always left out by the other children.

I wasn't the only one.

That changed everything.

Now, this in no way solved any of my problems, but it was a start. It was the turning point: the so-called glimmer of hope, when all hope should have been abandoned.

My life wasn't as bleak as it once was.

I knew Charlie Brown wasn't real. I was smart enough to understand that he was a character created by someone, but I also knew I had a lifelong friend in him. He accompanied me throughout my childhood and well into my adult years. He suffered with me in my sadness, kept me company in my isolation. I was the Pencil Pal he never met, the friend nobody else wanted to be.

In February 2000, my heart broke.

Mr. Schulz had passed. It was over. It felt as if Charlie Brown had died with him.

Eventually, I found out about Santa Rosa and visited the Redwood Empire Ice Arena. I sat in the Warm Puppy Café sipping hot chocolate, staring at the Snoopy painted on the walls, trying to picture Mr. Schulz sitting across from me with a cup of his own.

I visited the Charles M. Schulz Museum when it finally opened and saw his desk and chair on display. He once sat there and drew Charlie Brown.

Did he know he was drawing Charlie Brown for me?

I completed the trip by visiting Sebastopol, where he was laid to rest. I stood over the site, his marker within arm's reach, knowing this would be the closest I'd ever get to meeting him. I stood quietly as the rain continued to fall.

"What do I do?"

"What do I say?"

Anything I could say would have been inadequate to show just how much I appreciated this man.

Silently, I said good-bye.

Merrill Baker

I grew up an only child in a home where my parents constantly bickered. With all the arguments taking place, little time was left over for them to spend with me. My life was in constant turmoil, and my experiences at school were unhappy. Not having a brother or sister put me at a disadvantage as far as learning to relate to my peers. I wasn't the type to fight back when teased, so I became an outcast and had few friends.

At a very young age, probably around six, I was in the local five-and-dime with my father, when I begged him to buy me the single forty-five record "Snoopy vs. the Red Baron." From that point on, I was hooked. Initially lured by the music, I became a lifelong fan.

I used my allowance to buy *Peanuts* books, the collections of comics that appeared in the daily newspapers. I would close myself off in my room and read the books for hours. There, I found my friends. I could relate to Charlie Brown, who felt very alone and ostracized. But he had a circle of constant companions . . . and so, I thought, eventually I would, too. I saw that maybe it wasn't so bad being an only child. Who'd want a sister like Lucy? I learned from Charlie Brown that it's

okay to fail, but one's strength rests in getting up and trying over and over again, *despite* that failure. I was not a great student in school, but then neither was Peppermint Patty. She found her strength *outside* of school, on the baseball field.

I also attribute a lot of my independence to Charlie Brown and the *Peanuts* gang. The comic strip had no adults, so it wasn't so bad that I didn't have much guidance or adult presence in *my* life. I could get by on my own just fine. Like Charlie Brown, I could go anywhere and do anything, without having to be dependent on my parents to take me.

Like Snoopy, I could live my dreams and be whatever I wanted to be. Snoopy wouldn't settle for just being a dog, and he didn't let anyone keep him down. He took off for the wild blue yonder to fight the Red Baron, regardless of whether anyone believed that he actually left

the yard. He could also cook, argue a case, run away from home, and furnish his doghouse to the envy of any human.

Years later, when I drove cross-country to move to California, a friend bought me a Snoopy plush to keep me company. Snoopy rode in the front seat all the way from New York. As a child, I had purchased Snoopy stationery, key chains, glasses, and anything else I could find. Adulthood didn't change that. When Charles Schulz died in 2000, I felt it very deeply. It was like losing a lifetime companion. With his death, I feared the *Peanuts* gang would die, too, and I spent a fortune on vintage *Peanuts* memorabilia. Each piece makes me smile.

But as the years have passed, I've realized that the *Peanuts* gang has *not* died. They'll always live in my heart and my memories. They helped provide the stability and reassurance in life that I needed, and they contributed some happy childhood memories.

And now, with the perpetuation of the strip, they can be meaningful to future generations.

Denny May

I consider the comics in the daily newspaper as my dose of sanity, and I'm sad that *Peanuts* no longer runs in our newspaper.

Right from the start, I saw the *Peanuts* cartoons as a valuable source of wisdom. I delighted in the antics of the characters. In particular, Snoopy as a Beagle Scout was most appropriate, as I've been involved with scouting for the past sixty-four years. I used the wit and wisdom of Charles Schulz when training scout leaders. I injected humour into training situations and posted appropriate cartoons on the course bulletin board every day. I even hung a *Peanuts* cartoon in my scouting office: the one where Linus says to Lucy, "Every time there's a good suggestion, someone brings up the budget!"

I thought the Beagle Scouts cartoons always seemed to be "right on." The Beagle Scouts gave Snoopy opportunities and challenges, and Snoopy's "thoughts" were great. I remember, in 1980, when Harriet joined Woodstock, Conrad, Olivier, and Bill in the troop. Normally, that would have been shocking! Yet a few years earlier, a girl named Shauna joined our Cub pack. As always, Schulz was in tune with the world and reflected it in *Peanuts*.

But unlike Harriet, Shauna didn't bring along angel food cake!

Years earlier, I immediately thought of my Dad, the first time Snoopy appeared as a World War I Flying Ace on his doghouse. The memories came flooding back: of Dad's telling me how it was to fly a Sopwith Camel, how frightened he was when the Red Baron was on his tail, and how lonely it was in France in 1918.

I've always believed that Snoopy was, in fact, my Dad (W. R. "Wop" May), who flew a Sopwith Camel, and who, on April 21, 1918, outran the Red Baron and went on to survive the war. The song "Snoopy vs. the Red Baron" also makes me think: My Dad would have been number eighty-one, if the Red Baron's luck hadn't run out that fateful April day.

I was with my Dad when he died in 1952. He had a great sense of humour, and I know he would have enjoyed *Peanuts* and Snoopy as much as I do. I wonder where the story of Snoopy might have gone, once he donned an astronaut's helmet. I'm sure he would have gone on to Mars, where he would have discovered "Wop May Rock."

Snoopy flew for the first time in 1965, when my Dad had been gone for thirteen years. I wished I had asked him more, but I was just a kid when he died. I'll never know whether he "quaffed" a few root beers with a pretty French maiden. But he did tell me that he and his

Wilfrid R. "Wop" May in his Sopwith Camel, 1918

driver got in trouble when it took them *three days* to travel the sixty miles from the manning depot to the squadron.

I love sharing the stories about my Dad: his return to Canada in 1919, how he formed two airlines, trained pilots, flew mercy flights and the Northern Mail. I'm proud that during World War II he formed the Para Rescue Service and that he was honoured by the U.S. government in recognition of the many lives that were saved.

I have a sketch on my office wall, sent to me by Charles Schulz, of Snoopy on his doghouse, wearing his helmet and with his scarf fluttering in the breeze. I look at the sketch daily, and it always makes me think of my Dad.

I remember a cartoon where Woodstock shares a letter from his mom with Snoopy. "There's no reason for you to keep coming back to the nest on Mother's Day," the letter says. "That's not the way we birds do things! Once you've left, little bird, that's it! You can't go home again! So fly away! Don't look back! The world is yours!"

Snoopy's final comment is "I must admit she's a pretty sharp mother!"

It's obvious that Charles Schulz was a pretty sharp man.

Ellen M. Brenneman

As I look back through my life, I realize that almost every pivotal event has a memory of Snoopy painted into it.

As a child, I saw myself drawn into the world of a little boy named Charlie Brown. I easily identified with him: I was lonely, friendless, and uncomfortable in my own skin. But I strongly desired to be more like Snoopy, because he was so cool and confident. My earliest memories were of Sunday mornings, when my father read the *Peanuts* comic strip to me. My Dad worked terribly long hours, and this is one of my only memories of time with him at that age. Soon he gave me my first Snoopy, which began a lifelong love affair with the most cherished dog in the world.

I spent most of my childhood playing alone, because no other children lived in my neighborhood. Members of my family began giving me Snoopy items to keep me company when they'd come to visit. I became known as the "Snoopy Girl." My Uncle Clyde would often stop by a yard sale on the way to our house, and he always seemed to find a Snoopy in need of a new home. Sometimes this "new" Snoopy would be missing part of his ear or might be quite dirty, but I'd lovingly take him, clean him up, and introduce him with pride to the rest of my Snoopy family. I'd tell stories of what kind of life he must have led before being adopted into his permanent home. Every less-than-perfect Snoopy received this treatment, and I felt as though I were caring for orphans who needed mothering. I felt needed. Snoopy was my surrogate companion. He was with me when others could not be. He was a constant reminder of the people who cared.

One summer, as I played alone outside in the yard, my mother walked up to me while holding a package that had just arrived in the mail. I looked up as she said, "You looked like you needed some cheering up, so I wrote to Mr. Schulz a few weeks ago. I wanted him to know how much you loved his work and how important Snoopy is to you. Guess what . . . he wrote back!" She handed me the package. Inside was a lovely letter and the most beautiful book, called *Peanuts Jubilee*, and it was signed by Mr. Schulz. That was one of the most exciting days of my life. That book still is my most cherished possession: not just because Mr. Schulz was thoughtful enough to send it to me, but because my mother loved me enough to wish for happiness for her daughter.

I've grown away from the aches and pains of childhood, and as I reflect on my youth, I realize that my life is flooded with happy memories like the ones above. Every Snoopy in my collection is a token

of affection by those who have loved me. True, I've purchased some items myself. Most, however, have been given to me by family, friends, acquaintances, and even strangers. Whenever I feel down or lonely or have just had a bad day, I look at all these Snoopys, and all the good in my life floods into view. Every item is a joy, because each one chronicles my days, like a storybook. Some bring thrilling memories, while others bring sad ones, but they're all my life . . . as told by those who know me best.

I am the Snoopy Girl.

Andrea Podley

You never know what tomorrow will bring. You never know if your hopes and dreams—or things you couldn't possibly imagine—will happen to you. In a good way.

That's my story. At one time, I was married to a person who'd literally rip a *Peanuts* book out of my hands, tear it up, and yell at me for even *reading Peanuts* books. Needless to say, that marriage didn't last.

I met my present husband through an ad in a Los Angeles singles newspaper. Although my ad mentioned I was a boring woman, he seemed intrigued and wrote. No, wait, the fact that I shared his love of jazz got him to respond.

While we were dating, he noticed Snoopy seemed to be part of the decor of my place. He asked to see all the Snoopy items I had, and I took them out of a trunk and asked if he thought I was foolish. "No," he said. "You're a collector."

After less than a year, we decided to marry. He asked if I wanted an engagement ring. I wasn't into jewelry, and because it was the second marriage for both of us, I said no.

As soon as we were married, dear Phillip took me shopping . . . for Snoopy. He decided to make up for that diamond engagement ring, and every weekend we'd travel and shop for Snoopy. Each weekend I'd come home with a car full of Snoopys and the other *Peanuts* characters. I never met a Snoopy I didn't love.

When Phil realized that Charles Schulz was living and working in Santa Rosa, California, he made sure that I met him. He let the office know we were coming.

Phil marched me right into Mr. Schulz's office, at Number One Snoopy Place, and introduced us. Poor Mr. Schulz . . . he didn't know what hit him. But Phil was determined that I would meet him, and it was the first of many, many visits.

Right after that visit with Mr. Schulz, Phil was going through the mail one day. While thumbing through a collectors' newspaper, he said, "Look at this: Someone is starting a *Peanuts* collector club." "Shoot," I said, "*I* wanted to do that." Phil told me to look at the ad, and there was my name and address.

Phil had placed the ad for me, because he wanted me to meet and correspond with other collectors.

Girl loves dog; boy loves girl and gives her the world. With that ad, the world *did* suddenly open for me. I've met so many interesting, clever, and intelligent people, some who've become lifetime friends.

People who I've never met know about me from photos of my collection, which have been published the world over.

My husband Phil's ad in that collectors' newspaper was the beginning of the worldwide Peanuts Collector Club, which Mr. Schulz sanctioned, and which unites *Peanuts* fans and collectors. They realize they're not the only ones who collect The Beagle. The Club began in 1983 and continues to this day.

God spelled backward is *D O G*. I love both. And I truly love my husband, for all *his* love and support.

Tomoko Kuroda

The meeting between the *Peanuts* characters and me began after I met my husband.

Of course, I had seen some *Peanuts* movies and had a big poster of Charlie Brown before that, but only because they were "a story of a cute dog and a boy." I like cute characters.

When I met my husband, I was a bit confused to hear that he liked *Peanuts*. I wondered if it was okay for him to love these cute things as a grown-up man.

However, when he taught me about the charming children in *Peanuts*, and he also said, "Your profile looks a lot like Marcie," I fell in love with the characters. They felt so close to me at once. I'm not as bright as Marcie, but my hairstyle—and the line from my nose (with the glasses) down to my chin—looked a lot like hers then.

In those days, I had an inferiority complex about the line of my chin, but I gained a little confidence because I felt Marcie was my "other self."

Thirty years have passed since I met my husband, and the line of my chin has changed a lot with my age. But when I see Marcie as cute as always, it makes me smile to remember my younger days.

In December 2002, we attended a "Snoopy Christmas Tour" that visited places related to Mr. Schulz. We visited Santa Rosa, where the Charles M. Schulz Museum is; and Minnesota, where his father's barbershop used to be, and where Camp Snoopy still was (at the time). It was both a sightseeing tour and a trip that filled us with memories.

It wasn't long after he passed away, so everything we saw and heard at each place reminded us of his death. We were deeply impressed.

Since I like to draw, I decided to make a journal, to keep all these memories.

We had a very happy experience in 2007, five years after our first trip to Santa Rosa.

We happened to see the Japanese volunteer Miki Onodera, this time at an exhibition held in Tokyo and sponsored by the Schulz Museum. We first met Miki in Santa Rosa back in 2002, when she gave us a tour of the museum.

Miki became part of the journal I drew. I sent a set of copies of my journal to her, and she was pleased to receive it. And then, with help from Miki's son and some friends, even Mrs. Schulz got to see my journal. It eventually was posted on the Snoopy ice arena's Web site.

Although I drew the journal only for myself, to remember our trip, now it's like a dream that so many people can read it. There must be a wonderful power in *Peanuts*, which can connect all our hearts. Miki told me that this kind of joy is a "gift from Sparky."

I also believe that Mr. Schulz is watching us from somewhere, and that he still does happy tricks sometimes.

Sally Bennett Ryen

By 1959, Kennedy fever had hit St. Therese's Parish in Fresno, California, with a vengeance. Temporarily putting aside the task of springing souls out of purgatory, everyone in our family lit candles, said novenas, and added JFK to our nightly litanies, praying that he would be elected the first Catholic president.

My father's name being Jack, I demanded to know why my short-sighted parents hadn't named me Jackie, so I'd have one more thing in my favor when I met Caroline Kennedy, who was my same age and my best friend (although she didn't know it yet). How could I expect to be invited to White House slumber parties with a dumb name like Sally? I didn't know a single other Sally, which further convinced my five-year-old self that my parents had given me a loser of a name.

But my petulance and misgivings vanished in a heartbeat when I woke one morning in June of 1959. My family has always nurtured a love of comics, which continues to this day. Because my dad is an amateur cartoonist, we didn't just read the comics growing up; we studied the shading and lettering, discussed plot and characterization, and wrote fan letters to our favorite comic strip artists.

The entire previous week had been a breathless build-up as Charlie Brown awaited news from the hospital about the new baby. Boy or girl? And how would the *Peanuts* gang react to her? The payoff came on Tuesday, June 2. In the kitchen, I found my mom and dad laughing, the *Fresno Bee* comics page spread out in front of them and my older brothers.

My dad chuckled. "Wait till you see *this*," he said, a hint of triumph in his voice, and he picked me up and stood me on a chair. He pointed to *Peanuts*. There was *my* name, written in Charles Schulz's own handwriting, which we knew as well as our own: "Sally. Sally

Brown. Good ol' Sally Brown." Of all the names in the world, Schulz had walked into our family and chosen mine. I felt like I'd joined the cast of characters, curly hair and all.

I beamed at the thought of Caroline Kennedy seeing my name, for surely her dad read the comics to her every morning, just as mine did. I felt like a winner, as did Charlie Brown, who passed out chocolate

Sally, age three and a half

cigars heralding the arrival of his baby sister and basked in his new-found status as a big brother. My own big brothers, veterans at the ages of seven and nine, shook their heads, feeling a twinge of sympathy for Charlie Brown . . . and how his world was about to change.

My brother Jim sighed in solidarity for big brothers worldwide who are stuck taking care of little sisters. "Let's go play *Rawhide,*" he said to Peter. "Sally can be the prisoner." Adjusting his Zorro mask, Peter nodded. I climbed down off the kitchen chair, and the three of us headed single file down the basement stairs, not to emerge until someone either got hurt or hungry.

As usual, I was last in line, but I carried both the rope and a renewed faith in the world according to *Peanuts*.

Mary McKinney

He wore a blue jogging suit and had difficulty keeping the pants up around his belly. It was a late Saturday morning as he rested at the bar next to a glass of iced orange juice.

The bartender had a face as red as the Campari he drank while tending. He didn't mind a dog at the bar. In fact, he greeted Snoopy warmly and kept my orange juice coming.

I was eight years old and sitting, still in my soccer uniform, on a heavy oak stool at my dad's favorite bar. Shy as I was, I preferred to travel with security . . . that is, security in the form of a ten-inch stuffed beagle named Snoopy. His worn fur was closer in color to gray than white, and in place of his original nose, a fresh black pom-pom had been expertly attached by my mother. Where I went, Snoopy went, and this day and place were no exception. I needed him.

On the stool next to me, my eleven-year-old brother sat and played his football video game. My parents often brought us here, following our games.

In front of me, I could see bottles of all shapes and sizes: neatly lined up, brands facing out, filled with candy-colored liquids. Shiny, stacked glasses sparkled on the counter above the bottles, and the mirrors behind them reflected an empty restaurant. The staff was busy preparing for the weekend crowd, and soon the tables would be full.

I liked it best when we sat at the end of the bar, next to the garnish dispenser. This usually resulted in tiny plastic swords with maraschino cherries and orange slices in my glass. I liked listening to the waitresses chatting as they picked up and dropped off orders during lunch.

The presence of two children made some staff and customers uncomfortable. Some questioned my parents' judgment. Some felt sorry for us, and some felt that we were taking up stools that should

have been occupied by adults. Sometimes these comments reached my parents, but nothing changed.

We would be there for hours . . . about four beers, I think. My brother and I knew to be quiet, and that came easily for us. I passed the time by watching people, reading the bottle labels backward in the mirrors, learning cocktail recipes, and playing with my Security Beagle. I pulled his pants back up around his belly and evened the sleeve on each paw. I attempted to balance him in a seated position on the sloped, carpeted edge of the bar. I felt safe with him, because Snoopy could do anything, be anyone, and go anywhere. No matter what happened around me, I knew that I just needed to hold on to him, and everything would be okay.

Although going to the bar was routine, I never talked about it with my friends. I knew bars were strange places for kids to be, so I kept it a secret. I didn't want other kids to make fun of me, or know that I felt like I was different from them.

As the years passed, my family changed. My brother and I grew into adulthood, and my parents went their separate ways. Fortunately, for a long time now, my father's drink of choice has been coffee.

Through comic strips, cartoons, and greeting cards, Snoopy brought my family closer together and helped us express our feelings. Through all the insecurities in my life, Snoopy has provided happiness and security.

I know now that when I feel like Charlie Brown, all I need is a little Snoopy.

Heidi Rose

The March 17, 1967, issue of *Life* magazine featured an article about Charles M. Schulz, with Snoopy and Charlie Brown gracing the front cover. I was nine years old at the time, growing up in Southern California and caught up in the *Peanuts* craze, as so many kids were. I had always liked to draw, so naturally an artist would be my hero. The *Peanuts* characters were so likable and real, and I felt that somehow they were a lot like me. I admired Charles Schulz a great deal, because here was a grown-up who seemed to be sort of quiet and shy like I was, who liked to draw, and who was hugely successful at it!

I remember my mom reading the magazine article to me. I couldn't believe my ears when she got to this part: "Charlie Brown and his pals could live almost anywhere. But they are most at home at 2162 Coffee Lane, Sebastopol, California." I was amazed that his address would be announced for the whole world to know!

To me, Charles Schulz was on the same level as The Beatles, and I imagined the hordes of kids who now would descend on his home in Sebastopol. I wanted to be one of those kids, but since I had no idea where Sebastopol was—or how to get there—I decided to write Charles Schulz a letter.

In the letter, I told him a little about myself, and how—when I grew up—I wanted to be a cartoonist like he was. I drew several of his characters on little pieces of paper, slipped them in the envelope with my letter, and mailed it off. Only a few weeks later, a letter addressed to me—with a picture on the envelope of Snoopy lying on top of his doghouse—arrived in my mailbox.

I was stunned.

My dad carefully sliced open the envelope, and I excitedly read the typed letter to my family:

Dear Heidi:

Thank you for your kind letter and for your drawings. I enjoyed seeing them and appreciate your thoughtfulness in sending them to me.

Kindest regards,

Sincerely yours,
Charles M. Schulz

I remember how amazed we all were that the world's most famous cartoonist would take the time to write a letter to a little girl who sent him a few drawings. I have cherished that letter my whole life. It was the first, most significant encouragement I received in my dream to become an artist.

I pursued that dream, attended art school, and in the early 1980s I landed a job in the art department at Determined Productions in San Francisco, a licensing company for *Peanuts*. During that time, I wrote another letter to Charles Schulz, telling him of my job at Determined, and how he had inspired me to pursue my dream of becoming a professional artist. I received another response from him, this time through his secretary, Pat Lytle. In it, she said how pleased Mr. Schulz was to know that he had been able to provide some inspiration along the way as I came to realize my dreams and ambitions.

I will always remember Charles M. Schulz, not only for the characters he created, with whom I identified so well during my "growing up" years, but also for the way he inspired me to pursue my dreams through the simple gesture of an answered fan letter when I was nine years old.

Doug Ernst

In 1978, when my wife and I were struggling to quiet down our first baby at bedtime, it soon became obvious that she was happiest while being held, and that holding her parents hostage was part of her grand plan. That was fine and dandy for fifteen minutes, but at the end of the day young parents need their *own* quiet time.

We consulted various published baby experts, who seemed to agree that it was best for all concerned—baby and her parents—to teach the child that bedtime meant it was time to fall asleep. The trick, they said, was to help the baby feel emotionally secure, even when being separated from her parents.

Enter the stuffed animal.

We tried to give Sarah surrogate parents at bedtime: something to hug and cuddle while she calmed down long enough to realize that

she was tired, and to welcome the idea of sleep. We tried teddy bears, penguins, tigers, parrots, gigantic snails, giraffes, elephants, a monkey, talking fruit, animals that wiggled, kittens that purred and even baby dolls that were her size or larger.

Nothing worked.

In fact, these substitutes seemed only to remind her that they were not her parents. The bedtime problem continued to confound and frustrate my wife and me.

Then, one day, we gave her a stuffed Snoopy doll. It was big enough to hug and cute enough to put a little smile on her face. She was fascinated with his black nose. From that day forward, Sarah spent every night holding her Snoopy as she dozed off to sleep. She took Snoopy on outings and was comforted whenever he was nearby.

As she grew older, her three sisters received their share of stuffed animals, but nobody else got a Snoopy. There was a koala, a teddy, and a rag doll: Each was special in its own way, but Sarah knew her Snoopy companion was something else entirely.

Sarah held on to Snoopy well into adolescence and high school. When it was time to leave home as an adult, she packed him up and took him to her new home.

When it was time to have a child of her own, she made sure her son, Ryan, had his share of stuffed toys: dinosaurs, space creatures, lions, and cartoon characters of various shapes and sizes.

Just recently, my wife and I asked Sarah if Ryan was ever allowed to play with her Snoopy. Sarah gave us a quizzical look and quietly took us into her bedroom and pointed to the top shelf of her closet. There was her Snoopy: well out of the reach of her child—and most grownups—and packed carefully in its own plastic cover. Nearly thirty years old, he was very well used and clearly had earned his special space in her home.

And her heart.

Snoopy still sleeps with Sarah, safely, in his own bed. If she leaves the closet door open at night, she can see him smiling back.

And then she drifts off to sleep.

Sue Kreft

I can't remember when *Peanuts* wasn't a part of me. No special event or unusual item particularly stands out above the rest; the *Peanuts* gang has simply always been a part of the fabric of my life.

I've accumulated *Peanuts* books and collectibles over the years. I've had some for thirty-five years or more; others are more recent additions, particularly since Sparky died. I treasure one and all. They make me feel happy and special, no matter what is going on in my life.

In the 1970s, just out of college and teaching in a town 150 miles from home, I bought the set of four *Peanuts* Christmas cookie cutters and sent them to my mother, hoping she'd take the hint and make cookies for me. It worked! When her health was starting to fail and shopping for gifts became harder for her, I asked—with my birthday approaching—if I could have her *Peanuts* cookie cutters. (She had quite a few by then, mostly gifts from me.) That's when they came to my home, and I treasure them.

Today I sit, at nearly fifty-five years old, wearing sterling silver earrings that show Snoopy holding Woodstock ("dear little friend of friends"). I wear them often and don't care if others think I'm a little crazy. They make me feel special and unique. I have a matching charm on my bracelet. I don't wear that as often, because it's hard to type on a computer with a charm bracelet banging against the keys.

I have a Christmas tree with mostly *Peanuts* ornaments. Some date back to the 1970s; many are more recent. As I sit and look at my tree each Christmas, I realize how happy it makes me feel to see those ornaments, newly liberated from the boxes where they've been hiding all year. It feels like dear friends have come for their annual visit. I have a "*Peanuts* Christmas house." It doesn't feel commercial at all. It's warm and friendly, and a good place to be. During the past few years, since my sons left home and I've been alone, I've gradually decorated mostly with *Peanuts* ornaments. But we still have a family tradition of watching *A Charlie Brown Christmas* on Christmas night. It all takes me back to many good memories, both as a child and an adult.

During the past few years, a company has produced *Peanuts* fabric designs for the various seasons of the year. As a result, the "fabric of my life" has become a bit more literal. I made a jacket of the fabric that portrayed the *Peanuts* gang in the pumpkin patch; I wear it during most of October and feel quite cheered by it. I'm a quilter; eventually, I want to have a quilt for each holiday. So far, I have a Snoopy Valentine's Day quilt and a Snoopy St. Patrick's Day quilt, in the Irish chain pattern. A flannel Linus snowman quilt is next.

Now *Peanuts* truly warms my life.

One of the little square *Peanuts* books published years ago was called *Happiness Is a Warm Puppy*. To me, happiness is *Peanuts*: all the wonderful strips Sparky produced for almost fifty years, and all my special items that remind me of these characters and their many stories . . . unlike anything else ever drawn or written.

Even in sad or tragic times, my little friends are there to cheer me up.

Rob Kirby

The first thing that comes to mind whenever *Peanuts*, Charlie Brown, or Snoopy is mentioned isn't the comic strip at all; it's the jazz score brought to the cartoon show by the criminally overlooked Vince Guaraldi. I can almost hear it now. While I was just a little too young to have seen the formative years of the newspaper strip firsthand, I was completely hooked the minute I started actually reading our daily newspaper, the *Daily Mail*, when it plopped onto the mat sometime in the early 1970s.

In Britain, even today, you can still pay to get letter-box deliveries of your papers, so I'd try to prize that day's copy off my father as soon as I could, eager to read the next *Peanuts* installment, before looking over all the other comic strips, like Trog's all-but-forgotten *Flook*. But *Peanuts* always was the main treat of the morning. There was something so devastatingly simple about Charles Schulz's minimal use of lines to convey what actually was a highly detailed encapsulation

of childhood—complete with all its joys and sorrows, triumphs and heartache, love and indifference—that you simply had to come back for more the next day . . . and the day after that.

Without being childish, Schulz somehow captured that deep shard of innocence that most adults lose. Through this sacred crystal, he reflected his thoughts onto the printed page, perfectly capturing all the difficulties of the human condition from the eye-level perspective of a wonderfully drawn (in all senses) cast of individuals, particularly a little yellow bird and a dog that didn't act like any dog I'd ever seen before.

I first became aware of those colourful television cartoons by the middle of that same decade—possibly before I even discovered that a different Sunday newspaper we didn't get, the *Observer*, actually included a three-tier colour strip in their glossy supplement (weekly Schulz heaven!)—and that cemented my love for the adaptability of Schulz's cast of characters. They seemed to transition effortlessly from the static page to the moving image, thanks to the vision of Schulz, and the care and attention of a certain Mr. Bill Melendez and Mr. Lee Mendelson. The early shows, especially, also bound me even more closely to the characters, and Guaraldi's lilting, drifting music provided the perfect aural backdrop to those colourfully inky backdrops created for the show itself.

For me, all these elements were inextricably bound and perfectly balanced. But back on the printed page, Schulz didn't stop at the height of his initial success. He didn't let that success, and all the merchandising that came with it, go to his head; he was far too humble for that. He just kept on going, for nearly fifty years, rarely tiring; even as his hand grew shakier, he continued to challenge himself to reach ever-greater heights of expression. A half-century body of work is an astonishing legacy, and a deeply inspiring one.

As I began serious work on a reference book that eventually took more than seventeen years to complete, Schulz's example taught me that patience and perseverance do indeed reap dividends if you stick to what you believe in. But I'll never be able to make people laugh the way he managed to, every day, for the next fifty years.

That's a very special talent, and one that I'll treasure forever.

Cindy Cirucci Muders

My first Snoopy experience was back in 1972 when I was one year old, the youngest of four children. My mom's parents had gone on a trip out west, and they returned with gifts for each of us. My sister's gift from the trip was to be a Snoopy doll, and mine was to be a baby doll . . . but, as the story goes, I cried so hard for the Snoopy that the adults made the switch to keep peace in the land.

Initially, he was just Snoopy, and he and I were inseparable buddies for life. I carried him by the neck, which became very thin and made his head flop down. He had black, solid plastic eyes that our dog would chew out occasionally. My mom would sew them back in, teeth marks and all. Over the years, Mom had to re-cover Snoopy several times with new fabric, because he'd get so thin. I remember watching her sew quickly, so I wouldn't have to go too long without my friend.

I remember why I liked *this* Snoopy so much when I was young: It was the feeling of comfort. My pal, no matter what. As I grew into my teens, Snoopy just sat on my bed. By now, he was wearing pajamas, since his body was so thin. He was never re-covered again, instead remaining in a well-worn, much-loved state. When teenage problems would arise, I could still go to my bedroom and hug Snoopy. He always understood the problems of the day.

College came and went, and grown-up life began. I married and began living in a new home. Snoopy became "Old Snoopy" somewhere along the line: a term of respect and reverence. By now, I was deep into *Peanuts* collecting and had many new Snoopy items. My mom would say, "You still have 'Old Snoopy,' right?"

She and I would go up to my bedroom to find Old Snoopy on the dresser in his place of honor; she'd pick him up and laugh. She'd talk about how thin he was, how his neck flopped down, and how his eyes still looked chewed. She'd tell me the familiar stories of how my brother would hide him—in the dryer, once in the freezer—and it would take us hours to find him. We'd get a big kick out of remembering those days.

My husband and I just had our first child, and it's an exciting time. My mom still comes over; we still go see Old Snoopy and laugh. I realize now that the reasons why I love Old Snoopy have changed. Back then, it was purely comfort: a soft, furry friend who always made me feel better. Now, I look at Old Snoopy and see my family and all those good memories. I especially think of my mom, who worked tirelessly and lovingly: sewing eyes back in, re-covering Snoopy's fur, searching for him when he was hidden, and now asking about him so we can have some laughs.

Seeing Old Snoopy reminds me of the kind of mom *I* want to be: kind, thoughtful, loving, supportive, and generous with anything and everything.

So, dear Old Snoopy—keeper of secrets, comfort-bringer, constant friend and reminder of so many good times—thank you for your years of wonderful service and loyalty . . . and for the years to come. And thank you, as well, to Charles Schulz, who has brought such joy to my life and to the lives of others.

Kim Hunter Winemiller

Since I was a very small girl, *Peanuts* has been an important part of my life. When I was a teenager, I would cut my favorite strips out of the newspaper and glue them into an album. I would pull this out whenever I was feeling blue, and it always gave me a quick pick-me-up.

I was nine years old when my youngest sister was born, and we quickly came to refer to each other as Snoopy and Woodstock. When I was fifteen, our family was transferred to Switzerland for a year. My Snoopy doll flew with me on the plane—dressed in his Flying Ace outfit, of course!—and my baby sister carried her Woodstock doll. She even made each of them a "passport"; when we went through customs, most of the customs agents enjoyed the gag and actually stamped the passports for Snoopy and Woodstock. I still remember sending my Flying Ace through the "X-ray" machine at the airport and hearing the workers joke, "Here comes the pilot!"

While we were living in Switzerland, my best friend sent me several Snoopy greeting cards that used photographs of different places in Europe, with Snoopy "in" the scene. I was able to locate a few of these places and have my picture taken there, where Snoopy "had actually been." I remember carrying a greeting card around Venice, trying to locate the exact lamppost that had been used and finding it . . . and then proudly having my picture taken there.

As a teacher, I was able to pass on my love of Snoopy to my students. They're all grown now, and it gives me great pleasure to find that some of them are true Snoopy fans. I cannot count how many of my former students tell me they think of me every time they see Snoopy.

I'll never forget the morning I got the news that Charles Schulz had died. It still brings tears to my eyes. Valentine's Day would have been on a Monday, and I had mailed him a valentine to arrive that day. One of my first thoughts was "He won't get my valentine."

I never got to meet him in person, and it had always been my dream. Even when I was a teenager, my friends would wish to meet a movie or TV star, but not me! My dream was to meet Sparky.

He's still a part of my life. All my children are fans, and my youngest son's middle name is Charles, named after Sparky. My house is decorated with Snoopy in every room.

I still hope to spend time with Sparky someday. Ever since I was a kid, I've prayed that when I get to heaven, I could live next door to Charles Schulz.

And I just know that the Lord is saving that spot for me!

David E. Schmidt

I was twelve years old when I started to read Charlie Brown comics.

I couldn't wait until Sunday, to read Charlie Brown.

I used to wait for the holidays. My favorite ones were Halloween, Thanksgiving, Christmas, and Valentine's Day, when Lucy got kissed by Snoopy.

Lucy says, "Charlie Brown, you can kick the football."

He runs as fast as he can to kick the football. Lucy moves the football. Charlie Brown falls flat on his back.

I wear *Peanuts* sweatshirts and T-shirts, ties, sweatpants, and tops when we go shopping, or just to go out. I wear one of my ties to church.

After Thanksgiving, I wear one of my Christmas ties.

Whenever I go see this one doctor, he always likes to know if it is a new shirt, or if I had that one for a while.

Wherever I go, if it is shopping and I am wearing a Charlie Brown shirt, I say, "Oh, good grief, not again!" Everybody knows Charlie Brown is shopping in the store.

One Sunday in church, Mr. Don Fraser asked if I read Charlie Brown comics, and I said yes. Mr. Fraser and I have been friends for twenty-five years.

No matter how many times Charlie Brown loses, he keeps on trying.

Charlie Brown reminds me of myself.

Ellen Kent Beardsley

One morning, about eleven years ago, I saw Mr. Schulz sitting by himself in the Warm Puppy Café at the Redwood Empire Ice Arena in Santa Rosa. I wanted very much to approach him, to thank him and tell him how he and his characters had touched my life, but my sense of propriety and respect for Mr. Schulz's privacy talked me out of it. He passed away just a few years later, and—until now—I thought my chance to share my story had passed, as well.

My father, Earl Loyd Kent, was a huge *Peanuts* fan; he always read the daily comic strip and never missed a televised cartoon. He spent twenty years in the U.S. Army, so I grew up a "military brat," moving at least once a year from military base to military base throughout the 1960s and '70s. My special *Peanuts* story takes place in the late 1960s, when my family was stationed at Fort Benning, Georgia, and my father was serving in Vietnam on his one-year tour of duty. I was ten years old, living on a military base with hundreds of other families whose loved ones were engaged in combat overseas. The evening newscast and Walter Cronkite were a regular presence in many of our living rooms, as were the sometimes frightening photographs and film footage of the raging war.

Vietcong, Kissinger, Hanoi, POWs, troops, killed in action, peace talks, and *coming home* were words that I remember hearing often during this period of my life.

My fourth-grade teacher, Mrs. Santos, regularly had us write letters and cards that would be sent to the servicemen in Vietnam. My father was the lucky recipient of a stack of notes, drawings, and letters from my schoolmates. When my class received my father's return letter, I remember how proud I was to stand up and read it aloud to them.

My father wrote often to my mother, my sisters, and me; in anticipation of receiving something from him, checking the mailbox was one of the highlights of our day. One of the very first letters that we received had a very special drawing in it that we taped to our refrigerator: a very large drawing of Snoopy doing the "happy dance": the one where his head is thrown way back, arms outstretched, feet moving a mile a minute, a huge smile on his face.

But what made *this* drawing different was the unique "countdown calendar" that my father had drawn on Snoopy's belly. Each square on the calendar, which my sisters and I would cross out, meant that our dad was one day closer to coming home. Every time a square was marked off that drawing, Snoopy brought a bit of happiness and security to a war-weary and scared ten-year-old girl who desperately missed her Daddy.

Did Snoopy help bring my father safely home from the Vietnam War? Maybe, maybe not. But to this day, whenever I see Snoopy—especially when he's performing his happy dance—my heart is grateful and filled with loving memories of my Dad.

Thank you, Charles Schulz, for your gift to the world. And thank you, Snoopy, for the comfort and happiness you gave to me long ago and continue to bring me to this day.

Jay K. Payleitner

The annual all-school Christmas pageant was a month away, and Miss Triest's sixth graders at St. Peter Elementary School in Geneva, Illinois, pondered their options. In a brainstorming session, someone suggested *A Charlie Brown Christmas*, and the entire class unanimously applauded the idea. After all, this was 1968, and the *Peanuts* gang was riding a crest of popularity second to none. Sure, TV shows like *Laugh-In*, *Star Trek,* and *The Mod Squad* were regular favorites. But when a Charlie Brown special aired, you didn't miss it.

Someone brought the hardcover children's-book adaptation to class. A script was prepared, and auditions were scheduled for the next day. Most of the boys wanted to be Pigpen, and the girls were divided between Lucy, Sally, Violet, and Peppermint Patty. I set my sights on the role of Linus, and that night I did something that I'd never done before. I memorized a portion of the Bible, Luke 2:8–14. Seven verses! At the time, it never dawned on me that I was committing scripture to memory. I thought I was simply memorizing a long paragraph from the script that Miss Triest had handed out to us: one of those aromatic, bluish-purple documents freshly churned from a Ditto machine in the teacher's workroom.

Since then, I've tried out for dozens of plays, with decidedly mixed results. But that day, this twelve-year-old totally nailed his audition. I started with the words, "Lights please," continued with "And there were in the same country, shepherds abiding in the field, keeping watch over their flock by night," and finished with the memorable line: "And that's what Christmas is all about, Charlie Brown."

In addition to my stellar audition, it probably also helped that I was one of the shorter boys in the class and already had a Linus-style haircut.

The show was the hit of the pageant. As memory serves, we earned a thunderous standing ovation. Was it a turning point in my life? Perhaps. I was just playing a role, but as Linus I actually was sharing the greatest news in the history of the world. Something like that can have an impact on a preteen. Since then, my appreciation for the Bible, and committing a portion of it to memory, has greatly expanded. And

From left, future thespians Ed Stees, Jay Payleitner, Tim Dillon, John Hewitt, and John Nitkey

I have also been onstage a few times since sixth grade. As a producer for Christian radio and an author of several Christian books, I can even trace my chosen career back to that performance.

I haven't kept track of them, but I remember my fellow actors and the roles they played four decades ago: Tim Dillon as Charlie Brown; Cynthia Bachunas as Lucy; Christine Smith as Sally; John Nitkey as Pigpen; John Hewitt as Schroeder; Mary Strobel as Violet; and Ed Stees as Snoopy.

Thanks, Miss Triest.

Jennifer Prystasz

As a child in the mid-1960s, any money I received for birthdays or Christmas was religiously saved and used to buy the newest release by Charles M. Schulz. Once purchased, I'd curl up in a chair with my dad and read the book front to back, over and over again. Those dog-eared first editions, with my name proudly written in pen inside, form the basis of my still-prized book collection. They're my most precious collectibles. I wouldn't trade even one of them for a mint-condition duplicate signed by Sparky himself. I've never been sure whether my most vivid memory was the time spent wrapped up in my dad's arms, the distant echo of his tearful laughter, or the love of Snoopy.

In the early 1990s, still searching for books to add to my ever-expanding collection, I found an unusual one: *The Official Price Guide to Peanuts Collectibles*. The back page listed an address for the authors and the Peanuts Collector Club.

The Peanuts Collector Club? There were *others* like me?! I couldn't put pen to paper fast enough, and I received an equally speedy letter back from a woman who—unbeknownst to her—would soon change my life. That letter was from Club founder Andrea Podley. She and I quickly became fast and furious friends. Before I knew it, she had challenged me to create a forum to satisfy a new hunger: my desire for information about other collectors. "*Peanuts* People Pages" was soon born, a regular column in the Peanuts Collector Club newsletter. This column was dedicated to other collectors, all eager to share their particular passion for *Peanuts*. Not about their collections, but how this passion was born: what drove them to collect, along with special memories of their travels through life with Snoopy and the *Peanuts* gang. It was always incredible: Despite the diversity of these people, one common truth prevailed:

Charles M. Schulz and his drawings brought the world a little closer. We all had something in common, despite our other differences.

My favourite collectible isn't a music box, a book, a plush doll, a statue, or a piece of artwork; it's the memory of each and every collector I've ever met. Like my friend from Chicago, who sends a card on every holiday throughout the year and has done so for many years. Or my favourite Beaglefest roommate from New York, who sends a gift every so often just to make me smile . . . always at a time when I need that smile the most.

Or a friend from California, who sends my daughter her beloved Daisy Hill Puppy collectibles from around the globe. Or the most wonderful couple from Rhode Island, who send my daughters collectible U.S. coins each year as Christmas presents. Or my favourite collector from Ontario who, among other things, traveled to my hometown to offer support at my black belt grading.

Each collector I know adds another thread to the colourful tapestry of friendship that surrounds me, like a security blanket, in good times and bad.

Scott Alan Blanchard

My love for Snoopy, Charlie Brown, and the rest of the *Peanuts* gang began not long before my tenth birthday. One afternoon in September 1978, while outside riding bikes in Southern California with my sister and best friend, I suddenly got an excruciating headache. It was so bad that I asked my parents to cut my head off.

My parents gave me some children's aspirin and put cold cloths on my head, but that didn't help. They knew they needed to get me to the hospital, so they called for the paramedics. At first, the doctors didn't know what was wrong. They did some initial tests but found nothing to account for my headache. I was admitted and put on an IV sedative to calm me, but I pulled it out that night. The doctors knew something serious was going on.

The next day, my head was X-rayed and the doctors discovered I was suffering from an unannounced brain aneurysm: a mass of veins, arteries, and other stuff about the size of a golf ball. My parents were asked to sign the necessary paperwork while I was being rushed to the operating room, and the doctors gave them a *very* grave report: Basically, there was no hope for me. I ended up having three surgeries: one to remove the blood clot, one to remove the mass, and one to put in a plastic plate where my bone once was.

I needed a lot of help to get better and was moved to the Children's Hospital of San Diego. (According to the doctors, no one had expected me to even make it that far.) I became the "Miracle Boy" for everyone in the hospital, because I was doing so well.

I was still hooked up to wires the night before Halloween. My friends and twin sister came to visit in costume, and even the local TV news team was there. I saw myself on the local television newscast that night, just before watching *It's the Great Pumpkin, Charlie Brown.* I was tuckered out and had to go to bed right after the show . . . but that night is one of my first great memories of the *Peanuts* gang.

I was miraculously released from the hospital on November 22, 1978, the day before my tenth birthday. My next *Peanuts* memory is of the *huge* birthday cake the hospital staff made for me. The cake had a really nice Snoopy-hugging-Woodstock piggy bank. I kept that bank for a long time. It really meant a lot to me. Unfortunately, it broke many years ago, but it still has a place in my heart.

About five years ago, I found a bank that was similar to the one I had originally. I put any change from my pocket into it at the end of each day. I collect the change in that bank every November 22, and I make a donation to the local children's hospital, or to a center for research on neurological studies, to help kids in situations like mine. I like to think that maybe the money will be used to help some other kids start a love for *Peanuts* while they're in the hospital, as well as helping to find a cure or making their hospital bills less costly for their families.

Victoria Nguyen-Vu

I did not have Barbie, but I had you. I did not have Cabbage Patch Kids dolls, but I had you. I did not have summer camps, but I had you.

You came into my world during the summer of 1966, when our neighbor's son let me borrow his one-and-only prized copy of the *Peanuts* book.

Growing up in a neighborhood full of kids who often played together after school, I related easily to the *Peanuts* gang. I took an instant liking to the round-headed kid who served dinner while you smartly lounged on your rooftop. I often wondered if it was comfortable up there. I adored your eccentric personality. You were cool, Snoopy. Your petty arguments and protective manner with Woodstock always made me smile. You introduced me to the rhythm of American suburbia and showed me how other children played in another part of the world. Lemonade stands, psychiatric booths, baseball and the pitcher's mound, football, trick-or-treating, ice-skating, snow angels and catching snowflakes with your tongue . . . all were totally foreign in my neighborhood, and they totally captivated me and my friends. Your aerial combats with the Red Baron flew me away from the true combats broadcast on our radio. I forgot about the atrocities of war while reading about your attempts to reconnect with your mom at the Daisy Hill Puppy Farm. I found my own security with Linus and his reluctance to part from his security blanket. I patiently waited for the firing to cease each night, with Schroeder methodically playing his Beethoven right through Lucy's incessant sarcasm.

Then the rainy season started. I can still smell the earthy aroma of the soil and wetness, which soon was followed by the roaring rain that pounded on everything. Sheets of rain bent the trees, played staccato notes on the tiled roof, drenched the whitewashed walls, and gushed down streets lined with tamarind and other flamboyant trees. With the return of the rainy season, we all knew in our hearts that school was imminent.

This also marked your first experience with the monsoon, Snoopy. I tucked you and the *Peanuts* gang under my rain slicker and carried you to school with me. I also drew your likeness on the reverse of the brown paper bags that I used to cover my textbooks. I drew you everywhere: in my homemade scrapbook to share with my classmates, in my diaries, on posters in my room. I longed for your presence and wanted our pet dog to look like you. I put tennis shoes on his hind legs and held his front paws to guide him in Snoopy dance steps. Inevitably, gravity always got the better of him and he collapsed on

Thirteen-year-old Victoria, far right, with her siblings, from left, Kim, Dieu Chi, and Dieu Loan

all fours (to my big disappointment). When Mom brought home new, crisp white T-shirts for gym, my sisters and brothers helped me draw you dancing across the fronts. We stretched the shirts over a *Peanuts* book cover that pictured you dancing and carefully traced you in permanent Magic Marker. We started a trend. All our classmates were envious.

Snoopy, you colored my world and made my childhood a joy to remember. You shielded the sight of destruction. You blocked out the rumbling of bombs. You suppressed the cries of loss and mourning. You taught me the many ways to say "Happiness is . . ." Thank you for dancing in the days of my youth and introducing me to your gang. Thank you for being by my side through those unsettling times in good ol' Saigon. I hope you enjoyed the home I gave you far, far away from your birthplace.

Did I whisk you away from your world, or did you whisk me away from mine? Probably a bit of both, Snoopy, for you still dance in my heart, to the beat of a childhood filled with laughter and love.

Robin Dallin-Freyermuth

I grew up in Fresno, California. Due to the popularity of the *Peanuts* comic strip, a local department store—Rhodes—decided to have a Snoopy look-alike contest in the summer of 1966. The contest was meant for children and their pet dogs. After hearing about it, my parents helped me enter with my pet Bedlington terrier, Cocoa. Then, excitedly working with my Dad and Mom, I made a cloth helmet—using some old goggles my Dad had—and a beautiful turquoise satin scarf for my favorite pet to wear. We even wrote "Curse you, Red Baron" and drew a picture of Snoopy on the helmet, scarf, and goggles. I still have that scarf.

The American Kennel Club-sanctioned Sun Maid Kennel Club sent two judges to preside over the contest. The fun began with a very unusual assortment of colors, sizes, and breeds of dogs circling the ring. What a joyful thrill it was to hear them say, "Here comes the flying Bedlington," as Cocoa and I came prancing by.

Then they announced that we won first prize.

By winning, I got my first big bicycle—a blue-and-white three-speed Huffy—and a genuine World War I leather flying helmet. A friend of mine still has the bike to this day, and the helmet is a keepsake that my father treasures.

True, Cocoa wasn't a beagle. Being a Bedlington, she resembled a "little lamb," but with her helmet, goggles, and scarf on, she looked fierce enough to take on the Red Baron. (She looked more like Snoopy than the one beagle in the contest!)

That day, my dog got an added name—"Snoopy Cocoa"—and she didn't once object to wearing her helmet, goggles, and scarf. *She* knew who she was. She pranced all the way home while I rode my new bike. My sister was so jealous of my beautiful new bike that my parents had to buy her a new one, as well.

My love for dogs and other animals has only grown throughout the years. Since this episode, my many pets have always been "rescue" dogs and cats. At present, I have two wonderful mixed-breed dogs. Maybe they aren't from the Daisy Hill Puppy Farm, and Snoopy probably wouldn't claim them as siblings, but they would definitely be his friends.

Snoopy adorns our house in many forms, from treasured Christmas tree ornaments, to figurines, sweatshirts, and other memorabilia. Snoopy will always be part of my life.

I often look back to that hot summer day in August, in the big department store parking lot, and realize that—at that moment—my

Robin, age ten, and her dog enjoy the limelight with two contest judges

wonderful little dog and I really felt like Snoopy in his plane, with the wind in our faces, facing the Red Baron . . . and winning. As we showed off in the judge's circle—me on one end of the lead and Cocoa on the other—I felt like I was completely tied to Snoopy.

It will always be a treasured memory.

Beth Burkart

In our house, Snoopy is more than just a toy or a *Peanuts* character; he's a member of the family. It all started seven years ago, when my son, Jake, was a baby. He spotted our giant "New Year's Snoopy" on a high shelf in his room and wanted to hold him. Since then, Snoopy has seen Jake through some of the biggest challenges of his life, including new schools and day care centers, ear infections, an ear-tube operation, bee stings, and a broken nose.

Snoopy is magical: He simultaneously lives both in our house and in a place called Snoopyland. Based on Jake's fanciful tales, Snoopyland must be a magnificent spot that we'd all love to visit. Snoopyland even has a language called Snoopy language, complete with its own alphabet. Of course, Jake is the only human being who understands Snoopy language, so he has to translate for the rest of us.

Snoopy has the great fortune of enjoying multiple birthdays each year. From time to time, Jake announces that a particular day is Snoopy's birthday, and we're all invited to the party. In addition to people, attendees often include a subset of the other twenty-three stuffed Snoopys in our house. The party includes an elaborate plastic food buffet, and everyone brings a gift. All in all, our Snoopy has a pretty happy life and lives like royalty.

Snoopy has had many interesting experiences, both real and imagined. He has been lost twice. The first time was when, by accident, we left him on the roof of our car after a visit to the park. We next went to play at Jake's school and suddenly realized we didn't have Snoopy. When we retraced our steps, we miraculously found him in the parking lot of the city park: A Good Samaritan had placed him on the curb.

The second time Snoopy was lost was a lot more serious. Jake was in preschool, preparing to start kindergarten. In his preschool, the teachers had bent the "No toys" rule and allowed Jake to bring Snoopy with him every day. In kindergarten, he'd have to start leaving Snoopy at home. To ease the transition, I had begun to leave Snoopy in my car while I was at work, so he'd be there to greet Jake when I picked him up in the evening. One day in May 2005, I got off the BART train and headed through the parking lot to my car. I had a sinking feeling when I got to the appropriate parking space: My car was gone! I felt even more devastated when I realized that Snoopy, having been in the

stolen car, also was gone. How could we ever tell Jake that his Snoopy was lost? It was very sad, and we all thought we had seen the last of Snoopy. Jake used another Snoopy to go to sleep, but it wasn't the same. This one wasn't his best friend, just a look-alike.

Thanks to the police, my car was recovered in another city eight days later. As my husband, John, and I drove to the tow yard to examine the car, we hoped to find Snoopy, although we realized how slim the chances were. It was a thrilling moment when we discovered that Snoopy still was in the back where we had left him! Snoopy got a bath that day, and Jake and Snoopy had a most joyful reunion. Neither Snoopy nor Jake will ever forget this harrowing experience, and now they're even closer than ever.

Shari Noda

I have loved Snoopy and *Peanuts* since I was a little girl. Forty years ago, on my fifth birthday, I received the *Peanuts Cook Book* and a plush Snoopy dog from my Uncle Jimmy. Throughout the years, I've made recipes from that cookbook. Now I make these recipes with my own daughter and share the fun and memories with her.

My signature recipes are Lucy's Lemon Squares, Security Cinnamon Toast, and Lucy's Lemonade. I always wished that Peppermint Patty had made a Peppermint Whip instead of a Prune Whip, since I've always identified with her character (well, her looks, anyway!).

To this day, my Uncle Jimmy sends me *Peanuts*-themed cards for each holiday, with Snoopy stickers on them. I'm pretty certain my

Daughter Amy and Shari contemplate what to cook next

being a "foodie" and earning my home economics credential stemmed from having received this cookbook at an early age and cooking from it for more than forty years!

One of my adult dreams is to write an updated *Peanuts* cook book, to include a recipe for Woodstock's Fancy Millet Bird Treat, in honor of my pet cockatiel bird, Woodstock; and a Marcie's Marvelous Three-Mile-High Cake, in honor of my best friend, Liz, who is the spittin' image of Marcie.

I don't have my Snoopy dog any longer. I gave him to my son, Jacob, seventeen years ago; it accompanied him to many hospital visits, because he had five surgeries before he was two years old. During the final surgery, Snoopy got lost in the hospital bedding. I sort of felt like Snoopy became a "sacrificial lamb" that I didn't get to take home, because instead we got to take Jacob home, good as new!

I do still have my original Hallmark Christmas ornaments of various *Peanuts* scenes, which my kids love to hang on the tree each year. I still use my Snoopy address book with the Woodstock page mark, and I love to see the names and phone numbers of childhood friends and those of relatives who've long since passed on.

Much of my life has been lived using Snoopy products, and I'm happy that my kids can continue this tradition of loving the *Peanuts* characters.

Ed Glazier

In St. Louis, Missouri, in the early 1960s, our entire family was very fond of *Peanuts*; it probably was the one comic strip that we all read. One of our dogs was even named Snoopy. When Charlie Brown's little sister, Sally, was added to the strip, we enjoyed her antics tremendously, since my little sister also was named Sally. Every time the comic strip Sally was in the daily strip, we read it to see how much she was like my sister. Sally Brown's initial dislike of school (before she started) and her change of heart (after she entered kindergarten) very much paralleled the way my sister, Sally, had behaved.

My sister Sally's birthday was coming up one year, and my mother was planning a birthday party for her. My sister must have been about twelve. (She was born in 1951.) I don't know whose idea it was, but we had a brainstorm and decided to have a *Peanuts*-themed party for her. But this was before commercially licensed *Peanuts* party decorations were readily available, so we decided to make our own. I made place cards by tracing *Peanuts* characters from the Sunday strips (they were larger), and I hand-painted them. My sister had had a rubber Snoopy toy for a couple of years, and this inspired my centerpiece design: I made a doghouse out of a cardboard box, and I managed to tape the rubber Snoopy to the doghouse, to imitate Snoopy's favorite resting place. On a large piece of wrapping paper, we made an outline of Snoopy; instead of "pin the tail on the donkey," we played "pin the tail on Snoopy."

We were proud of our creativity, so we wrote to Charles Schulz and described the party, the decorations, and the game. My sister was soon surprised to receive two *Peanuts* cartoon books in the mail: *Snoopy* and *You Can Do It, Charlie Brown*. The frontispiece of *You Can Do It, Charlie Brown* has a picture of Snoopy in the outfield, wearing a baseball cap and a baseball glove. An even bigger surprise was the way Mr. Schulz kindly signed the page: "For Sally with best wishes for a Happy Birthday—Charles M. Schulz." In addition to the greeting, he drew a "thought balloon" of a birthday cake, plus the addition of a tongue on Snoopy, who then appeared to be licking his lips while thinking of the cake.

A few years later, in 1966, when I was an undergraduate at Michigan State University, the campus newspaper (the *State News*) published a cartoon parody of Snoopy chasing the Red Baron. I sent this cartoon to my sister, and she sent a copy to Mr. Schulz. He wrote back: "Thank you for taking time to write and send a copy of the cartoon

from the *State News*. Many readers have sent drawings of Snoopy pursuing the Red Baron, but this is one of the funniest I have seen yet." My sister kept his letter with her other Schulz gifts.

These were favorite possessions of hers, and when she died an untimely death in 1992, I found these books among her belongings. I still have them as mementos of my sister.

Adam Bonner

I received my first Snoopy stuffed animal for Christmas when I was three years old. I'm thirteen now, and I still sleep with that Snoopy every night. I'm an only child; Snoopy is my brother, my sister, and my pet. He's as important to me as my parents are. He has a new nose because I chewed the original one off; he's not as round anymore, because I've slept on him many times; and he's losing his fur in a few places, because I've given him lots of hugs. But he has meant everything to me . . . especially when my parents were going through a divorce.

Over the years, I've accumulated many Snoopy collectibles. My bedroom is filled with Snoopy items won on eBay, purchased during two trips to the Mall of America, and found at other stores that my

parents and I shop at. But that first Snoopy is the one that means so much to me.

Snoopy would sit on the floor whenever our family played board games. He would sit on the windowsill and look out at us when we played in the yard. Sometimes, he'd sit at the kitchen table during a meal.

We even celebrated his birthday every year. My mom would bake him a cake, and I would decorate it; then we'd sing "Happy Birthday" to him. I even wrapped gifts for him. Snoopy always went on vacation with us, and sometimes my dad would let him pretend to drive the van.

Whenever I get sick, Snoopy is right next to me to make me feel better. When I watch a sad movie, Snoopy wipes the tears off my face. My dad and I have always felt that those tears give life to my Snoopy.

I know I'm 13, but my Snoopy means as much to me as Linus's security blanket does to him.

A few summers back, my mom told me that I was too old to sleep with Snoopy. She said that I needed to grow up, and that my Snoopy needed to be placed in a corner in my bedroom and left alone. She even went so far as to throw him out the window one day.

Needless to say, I was very sad and quickly ran outside to get him.

My dad, knowing that I was upset, took me on a special vacation to Santa Rosa, California, so I could visit the Charles M. Schulz Museum. Snoopy went with us, of course—stowed in my backpack—and even got into many of the pictures we took.

While we were at the museum, we were lucky enough to meet Jean Schulz. I showed her my Snoopy, and she thought it was my dad's, from when he was a boy. I told her my mom thought I was too old to have Snoopy, and Mrs. Schulz told us a story about a man in the military who sent Charles Schulz a letter about how he took a plush *Peanuts* character with him to make him feel more comfortable.

She told us that *nobody* is too old for *Peanuts*.

Joan Wernick

I'm afraid to say this, but in September 1968 I knew nothing about Snoopy. Well, maybe I knew he was a cartoon character. But not much else.

I had recently graduated from Boston University and had gotten my very first teaching assignment. Mid-August I drove to my school to meet with the principal. I was ushered into my classroom and told I had a large bulletin board that I needed to keep updated.

During a trip to the local teachers' store, a saleslady suggested using holidays or seasons to decorate my bulletin board. After wandering somewhat aimlessly up and down the aisles, I did neither. I bought a big yellow school bus and decided it would look welcoming with every child's name on it. As the other teachers gradually returned, I felt good about my choice; many seemed to have the same cutouts on *their* walls.

Then the children arrived.

Although I liked my big yellow bus, the children weren't exactly enthralled. Perhaps it was because the other teachers had decorated not only their bulletin boards, but also their walls.

During the second week, a boy asked if he could talk with me. He and his friends were bored with yellow busses, apples, and leaves. Clutching a black-and-white beagle, he asked if I'd hang it up. I asked if the dog had a name. He looked incredulously at me and responded, "You don't know who Snoopy is?" The following silence seemed to last forever. "Of course," I finally said. "I'll hang him up."

The boy suggested the front door was the place, because everyone would see him. So up he went: my very first Snoopy.

It wasn't long before other children followed suit. Halloween was coming, and I had put up pumpkins. They soon were replaced with hand-drawn Snoopys, Hallmark Snoopys, and other Snoopys. Gradually, my school bus vanished. The Snoopys seemed to be multiplying. One time we actually counted them. We stopped at two hundred!

As the years passed, I developed something of a reputation: I became the "Snoopy teacher." I had found my theme.

During the course of my teaching career, I've switched schools and classrooms, but the one constant has been Snoopy.

Every year, my first-grade class celebrates Snoopy's birthday. They're greeted by a *huge* Snoopy display from a Hallmark store. For that one day, we do no work; we just celebrate the beagle.

Our morning begins with two art projects. The first is sponge-painting Snoopy's face. The second is a Snoopy quilt. Each child creates two .quares: One has Snoopy's face, and the other has a checkerboard design using red, black, and white squares. Parent volunteers glue everything together and then it's proudly displayed on the hall bulletin board.

After lunch, we have a Snoopy show-and-tell. The children bring any Snoopy item they wish to share, and I bring a few items from my ever-expanding collection. The children always are amazed at my items. I'd say the Snoopy hair dryer gets the most *oohs*. However, a close second would be my attire for the day: Snoopy jeans, shirt, jacket, bow biters on my shoes, earrings, necklace, and watch!

This is followed by a showing of *Snoopy's Reunion* and a party. Some mom always makes a Snoopy cake that just leaves us all speechless.

Long after the children have learned to read and completed their final math tests and science experiments, they remember Snoopy's birthday.

Forty years later, I'm still teaching. Snoopy has brightened the walls and hearts of countless first graders, who all look forward to being the only class in school to celebrate Snoopy's birthday as a national holiday.

And to think it all began with a six-year-old boy who thought my walls were boring.

Gaylord "Hap" Hill

I've been a fan of the *Peanuts* gang for as long as I can remember.

I was often called Charlie Brown myself. During my many years in the navy, I always sent *Peanuts* cards for birthdays and special events to my youngsters and close friends. Even now, my desk is adorned with Snoopy mementos.

During my naval career of flying, I read the newspapers each morning, always finishing with Charlie Brown and the gang. I always got airborne knowing that the *Peanuts* gang was there with me. And when I had "shore duty" in Washington, D.C., it was almost the same. I made *Peanuts* required reading, each morning, for those in the office with me. We always started with a chuckle and a smile.

The highlight of my association with *Peanuts* came in the mid-1960s. At that time, I was a commander on the staff of naval air force, U.S. Pacific Fleet. I knew that I soon was to be considered for promotion to the rank of captain. And if I made it, custom required that I had to have a promotion party: a "wetting down" party. I looked for something unique to use as an invitation. I decided to check with Charles Schulz, and I "roughed out" an idea while waiting, hopefully, for a good word from Washington.

When that "good word" came, I got on the phone with Mr. Schulz and requested his *Peanuts* gang for my invitation: "Mr. Schulz, don't hang up on me! I'm calling you from cloud nine over San Diego!"

I explained what I wanted for the special invitation. At first, he thought I wanted to use the characters.

"No, sir," I answered. "I'd like you to draw them."

It must have caught him by surprise, because he admitted that he didn't understand what I wanted.

"Sir," I said, "I have it all roughed out, right here in my hand. I'll put it in the mail to you this afternoon."

A couple of weeks went by. I was catching some flak about being the "cheap captain," because I hadn't scheduled the party. I had to set the date. Then, to my thankful surprise, the drawings came back:

"Happiness Is a Fourth Stripe!"

We printed a few hundred copies. My two daughters, Gayle and Lynne, hand-colored the invitations in the Sunday *Peanuts* colors.

That invitation became a collector's item. I later saw them framed and hung on office walls. I even received requests for extra copies of this "wetting down" party invitation, all thanks to Charles Schulz.

It was a gala event: a truly memorable affair.

Jason A. Scalese

I'm the assistant men's tennis coach in charge of fund-raising at Sonoma State University, and I work for the Santa Clara University tennis team. I also coach high school tennis and work for the U.S. Tennis Association in Alameda.

I live in Burlingame with my wife, Tamra, and dog, Summer.

I was born near Boston and was considered just a step above legally deaf. I was born with an outer ear deficiency, as well . . . which, needless to say, got me started in life with some insecurity. After a few years of failing to find any doctors who could help me in the New England area, my parents were alerted to two doctors working out of Stanford University's California Ear Institute.

One doctor was an outer ear specialist, who had reconstructed the ear of J. Paul Getty's grandson after he was kidnapped and had his ear severed. My father read this story in *Time* magazine. At the time, my parents' insurance did not cover the expenses necessary to literally reside in California for multiple months at a time, to have the necessary surgery to fix my hearing and reconstruct my outer ears.

The money was raised with the help of the Plymouth (Massachusetts) Lions Club, and off to Palo Alto we went. After the two doctors assured my parents that they could help, I had my first surgery. It lasted twelve hours, during which I was given a donor eardrum and inner ear bones, and a new canal was built. Nothing was done on the outside; that was planned for later, after my growth had stopped. (Remember, I was only five years old.)

After an exhausting day, my parents were relieved and thankful that my hearing was improved to near perfection in one ear. I'd never need to wear a hearing aid again.

The following year, I was brought back for further widening of the canal that had been built, along with what was expected to be the beginning of the work on my other side. Prior to the surgery, a friend of my parents had assembled a gift pack for me to take on the trip. (It was near Christmas.) One of the gifts was a stuffed Snoopy.

It was a typical Snoopy plush doll. It came with several costumes, one of which was of a doctor. I apparently became quite close to that Snoopy, and I had it dressed as a doctor when I went in for my second surgery. I refused to give it up while going into the operating room, and my parents insisted I be allowed to keep it. The doctors agreed.

My mother reminded the doctors that I had scared them by hyperventilating after my previous surgery. Taking precautions, they arranged for a cardiologist to be on staff during my operation. It was a good idea: Two hours into my surgery, I went into cardiac arrest. Several recovery efforts failed, and finally I was injected with a medicine to counter the anesthesia . . . and I survived.

Later, I was diagnosed with malignant hyperthermia, a syndrome in which people are allergic to general anesthesia. At the time, in the early 1980s, only a couple of hundred cases worldwide had been reported. The doctors agreed that my mother's information about my earlier hyperventilation had saved my life, because the cardiologist had been exposed to MH before.

Now, I won't say that anyone in my family believed Snoopy was watching over me at the time, although we've often joked about it. What *is* important, though, is that I'm now thirty-three years old . . . and Snoopy is still with me.

I've always claimed that his importance is not that he saved my life, just that he was there.

As a tennis player, I'm highly superstitious. That trend has continued in other areas of my life. I do not travel on a plane without Snoopy. I've had three surgeries, and each time I've insisted Snoopy be with me. While he doesn't sleep in bed with my wife and me, he does sit up on a dresser overlooking the room.

I don't frequently attend church, but I've always felt Snoopy is, in some way, my guardian angel.

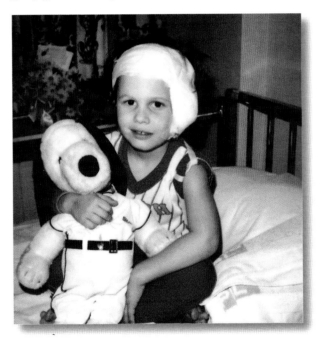

I wrote this because Snoopy has been important to me my entire life. I'm sure people will write about the importance of the comic strips, and like many I've enjoyed them and the TV specials through the years.

But my Snoopy doll is my most priceless possession.

Jeremy E. Grossman

An anonymous librarian changed my life forever by introducing me to my oldest and dearest friend: Charlie Brown.

The children's department of our local library offered a unique program: The staff would put together a care package of books, magazines, and records for a child who was sick, so he or she could have things to read and do while home from school. On one such occasion, when I was home ill, my mother telephoned the library and picked up the bag of goodies a short while later and brought it home to me.

As I sorted through the bag of various library resources, I found something unexpected: a rather tattered book with a faded cover that was held together with red library binding tape. The book was *Go Fly a Kite, Charlie Brown*, and it was the first collection of *Peanuts* comic strips I had ever encountered. In fact, at that young age, I had no idea such books even existed. I remember telling my mother about this amazing, remarkable book and how it actually had Charlie Brown comic strips in it!

Up to that point in my life, I had only observed Charlie Brown from afar, in the highly anticipated annual airings of *A Charlie Brown Christmas* and *It's the Great Pumpkin, Charlie Brown*.

Now, I no longer had to wait to see Charlie Brown!

After that eventful day, I quickly devoured every book our library had that featured good ol' Charlie Brown, Snoopy, and the rest. I spent hours in my bedroom, reading and rereading these collections. I felt constantly frustrated by the library's limited collection and was filled with excitement when a *Peanuts* book arrived that I hadn't read before. I eventually grew to love all of the "*Peanuts* gang," but Charlie Brown always was first in my heart.

I got to know Charlie Brown through these books, and as I came to know him, I realized how much we were alike: misunderstood, shy, clumsy at sports, frustrated by our failures, and desperately wanting to be liked. All the kids in my neighborhood had moved away by this time in my life; growing up was indeed very lonely. And even when kids my age *had* been around, my story was much like Charlie Brown's: always the outsider looking in, or a second fiddle.

As a child, reading about Charlie Brown's anxieties and feelings helped me cope, as I struggled with many of the same problems he had. No matter how bad things may have seemed, there was comfort in knowing that I wasn't truly alone; someone else was going through the same things.

As an adult, I've come to understand that there's a little Charlie Brown in all of us: a universality that made *Peanuts* a success, and

a reflection of the mastery of Charles Schulz himself. We've all been comforted to know that no matter what our struggles, fears, or anxieties, Charlie Brown has faced them with us.

Yet this sharing of Charlie Brown with the rest of the world doesn't detract from the special bond between him and me. Charlie Brown will always be my friend: a friend who can only listen but still speaks to me in the deepest, most sincere ways.

I've enjoyed few things as much as I've enjoyed the sequential release of *The Complete Peanuts*. I'll be almost forty years old when the final volume is published, and Charlie Brown will be pushing seventy (and still not looking a day over eight!). Rereading these comic strips—starring good ol' Charlie Brown, who always was there for me, who always knew exactly what I was going through and what I was feeling—is like a reunion with my oldest and dearest friend.

I've treasured every moment.

Christine Nohr

Peanuts—but mainly the beagle with the big nose—has been a major part of my life for more than forty years.

If I had to say how it started, it must have been when I was a very young girl and was sent to a weeklong summer camp where I knew no one. I was rather shy and not the adventurous type, and I missed home and my mom like crazy. My first plush Snoopy came with me to camp, and he got me through it . . . and to say we've been inseparable ever since would be an understatement. That well-worn Snoopy, even more loved than the Velveteen Rabbit, is in a keepsake trunk; his replacement, now thirty-three years old, has been all over the country with me, on vacations and other trips.

The best example I can give of Snoopy's role in my life goes back about twenty years, when I brought him to a doll hospital to be cleaned and to have his floppy neck restored. I was about to go on a vacation and was very disappointed and worried when the doll hospital told me they wouldn't have him ready before I left. I had visions of him getting lost or being given away to the wrong person. Unbeknownst to me, my husband had gotten in touch with the doll hospital, and he told them Snoopy *had* to be ready before we left. My dear, sweet husband secretly picked him up and brought him home the night before we were to leave. When I finished work that day, there was Snoopy: white as snow, his neck fixed, and wearing a big red bow. I was thrilled: Needless to say, there were tears of happiness. I was then able to go on vacation without worrying about Snoopy.

The funny thing was that the doll hospital had rushed to get him ready, and they forgot to sew his toenails back on after washing him. As a result, my Snoopy—unlike all others—has no black lines on his feet. I've kept him that way as a reminder of his hospital stay.

The spirit of *Peanuts*, and the wonderful and amazing personality Charles Schulz gave Snoopy—which resides in this stuffed animal— mean so much to me. I think we all recognize a part of ourselves in one *Peanuts* character or another. I love them all, but Snoopy has always been special. He's so much a part of me that I think my two teenage children think of him as their older sibling . . . just smaller and fuzzier. I guess it's only fitting that the woman who was my children's nanny when they were young got the job mainly because we discovered we were both total Snoopy lovers.

When Charles Schulz passed away, I grieved and truly felt as though a member of my own family was gone, or as if Snoopy's "dad" had died.

I'm a collector now, but it's not about the "stuff." It's about the joy, tears, laughter, and warm, fuzzy feelings that Snoopy and the *Peanuts* gang bring me. I imagine that when I'm a grandma in a rocking chair, Snoopy will be right beside me . . . and I'll be busy turning my grandchildren into *Peanuts* fans.

Tracey Dukert

For as long as I can remember, going to my grandfather's house meant visiting the gang that knew the most about him. They were two-dimensional kids who lived inside a comic strip: the *Peanuts* gang. They understood how he felt about friendship, they knew why his dog was his best friend, and they were the best at making him laugh. For this reason, I looked forward to walking into my grandfather's kitchen for more than twenty years, to check out his refrigerator: not for food, but for the newest *Peanuts* comic strip he had taped to its door. Every time I visited, a new one was displayed. My grandfather often explained to me why each *Peanuts* comic strip meant something special to him. He could find a hidden "personal" meaning in every one of Charles Schulz's daily creations; in return, I learned much about my grandfather that nobody else would ever know.

I specifically remember one of my grandfather's *Peanuts* comic strip posts, in part because it was the one on his refrigerator at the time of his seventy-fifth birthday and also because he associated it immensely with the witty actions of my sister and me. It was an historic, winter-themed sketch. Snoopy and Woodstock were dressed in military attire, frigidly guarding General George Washington's log cabin. When asked to find and cut firewood for their general, the two willingly departed their guard duty to begin the search. After realizing that this would require cutting down trees larger than the general's log cabin, Woodstock suddenly had an idea, typically noted by the multiple lines of "birdspeak" inside a thought bubble. Upon the duo's return to Washington's log cabin, Snoopy spoke for Woodstock and recommended that the general simply turn up his thermostat.

My grandfather loved this one, and he knew I did as well. It was the simple, brilliant smile that Snoopy and his miniature sidekick could bring to his face at any moment. My grandfather compared these two to my sister and me quite often, noting this comic strip as a perfect example. When we were very young, I was given a plush Snoopy; my sister received a plush Woodstock. They went with us on all our journeys. To my grandfather, this surely was a constant reinforcement of his amused comparison. My sister and I were—and forever will be recognized as—the Woodstock and Snoopy of our family: the entertaining duo leading quite comical lives.

My Snoopy plush lives on my living room chair today, and he brings a smile from ear to ear when I see him. I admire my grandfather's simple love of laughter: something so hard to observe these days.

Later in life, I realized that this specific comic strip was important because it reminded him of his grandchildren, who meant so much to him. When my grandfather passed away in August of 2006, I held on to his tradition. Now *I* post a meaningful *Peanuts* comic strip on my refrigerator door. To me, the gang has illustrated everyday values, reminded me to laugh, and—most important—kept someone in mind who means so much to me.

Shano P. Rodgers

I always loved the *Peanuts* characters and comics, so when my high school did a production of *You're a Good Man, Charlie Brown* during my senior year, I jumped at the chance to play my favorite, Lucy.

Like Lucy, my fatal flaw was falling in love with the boy who played Schroeder. And, like Schroeder, he had absolutely no interest in me. I pined for him and was totally devastated when he asked another girl to the prom.

I managed to move on, still identifying with Lucy. Ironically, years later I obtained my master's degree in clinical psychology. To this day, I have a figure of Lucy in her psychiatric booth sitting on my desk.

But I never forgot the boy who played Schroeder, and my unrequited love for him.

I originally had no intention of going to my twenty-year high school reunion. I hadn't gone to the ten-year event, and as I had just taken a business trip to London earlier that month, I felt that I couldn't spare the time away from work. But my sister and a couple of high school chums convinced me to make the trip back to Colorado.

When I walked into the gathering, I saw my "Schroeder" almost immediately. He saw me, too, but didn't say anything. I said, "Okay, Fred, you either don't recognize me, or you're blowing me off again."

Turns out he *did* recognize me. We got to know each other again that weekend. Neither of us had married, and we were both very much on the same wavelength.

I flew back to California with a renewed sense of hope, having discovered that my feelings hadn't changed. I dared not hope that he felt the same way, but he called me every day after that. We spent hours on the phone, and it wasn't long before he came to visit. Six months later, he spent Christmas with me.

The last gift I opened from Fred that Christmas Day was a toy. A Post-it note was affixed to the front of the package, with a Lucy sticker on it and a clue to a scavenger hunt throughout my apartment. Each subsequent clue had stickers of the *Peanuts* gang.

The final clue displayed a sticker of Lucy and Schroeder at the piano and led to the discovery of my engagement ring.

We were married a year to the day after our twenty-year reunion. The groom's cake featured prominent plastic figures of Lucy gazing fondly at Schroeder as he played the piano.

Our motto "Miracles happen" clearly illustrates that however unlikely and against all odds, this particular Lucy and Schroeder ended up together.

Joe Patane

In 1971, when I was about one year old, I received my first plush Snoopy, who remains with me to this day. As the last of eight children of a dedicated flight engineer for Pan American World Airways, I didn't see my father much and was generally left to my own devices for entertainment; I was "too little" to play with my seven older brothers and sisters. Well, many years of creative-time-passing ensued, with me trying to be like my plane-flying dad by pretend-flying my own "SuperSnoopy" all over my triple-bunk-bed room, serving the passengers whatever they needed, and so forth. There wasn't a whole lot of space to do all of this, since three of us boys slept in one room, and three girls in another, with the two oldest downstairs somewhere.

Family members would generally see me running up and down the stairs to achieve my airline's cross-country or (on special occasions) international routes. To make me stop the noise and distraction, some of my brothers and sisters would tease me away from them. They'd sing all kinds of parody songs like "Joey did pee-pee in the poo-poo pot"—and much worse—generally sending me crying into my room, with an unmanned SuperSnoopy aircraft at my side.

It was a typical Italian household, I suppose, with everyone picking on (and bickering with) each other . . . especially me, since I was the smallest. Snoopy always was there for me during these beratings . . . and during my brothers' fistfights, my sisters' times of the month, my parents' frequent "grown-up" arguments, and more. Snoopy let me retreat to him, hold on to him, cry into him, and even share my first kiss with him. We really did it all. He truly was my best friend. I was generally a nerdy kid, and while my brothers and sisters went on about their "grown-up" lives and hung out with their "important" friends, it was just me and Snoopy. I didn't need anyone else, just Snoopy and my imagination!

To this day, if I need a little boost or smile to brighten my day, I just take SuperSnoopy out for a flight around my home—my *own* home now—and my daily troubles just seem to melt away.

My dad recently passed away at the ripe age of eighty-seven, and I was as sad as could be, but he gave me and my family great opportunities and support through it all. A week or so after Charles Schulz passed away, he was to present a "Best Little Actress" award to a great friend of mine in California. It finally was my chance to meet the man who put a lot of spring and pep in my life through his comic strip. Well, I was devastated when he passed, so I mourned for days that I hadn't reached out to him sooner. Even so, I managed to pick myself up and get to the special event just the same. To my great surprise, Bill Melendez—who animated the *Peanuts* television specials—spoke in place of Mr. Schulz,

and it was one of the most amazing hours of wonderment in my heart and mind. The stories he told about him and Sparky were so special, so meaningful, so beautiful. After Mr. Melendez completed his speech, several people helped him to his chair, where I nervously presented myself as a huge fan, both of his speech and all of his work with Sparky. Well, imagine my amazement when he told me that he was the voice of Snoopy! He also took the time to draw a personalized sketch of Snoopy for me on Schulz's biography page in the program. I was in awe!

I've learned much from Snoopy's multifaceted personalities: Flying Ace, French lover, sophisticated eater, writer, dancer (*Flash Beagle* was one of my favorites!), devoted friend, and more. At one awkward time, I even grew and developed my very own—and relatively misunderstood—personality inspired by Joe Cool. (To this day, I suffer repercussions from that!) Snoopy is just so colorful yet remains so simple. I wanted so much to *be* like him. I loved cookies and root beer because of him. I yearned for family because of him, thanks to the movie *Snoopy, Come Home*.

Eventually, I learned to love unconditionally because of him.

Sallie M. Mugavero

It has been with me most of my life.

It started out bright blue, soft and smooth to the touch. I spent roughly eight to ten hours each day with it. It's now faded blue, paper thin, and has those little fuzz balls on it: my Snoopy pillowcase. I finally retired it four years ago.

I'm now twenty-nine years old.

I've loved Snoopy and the *Peanuts* gang for as long as I can remember, and I've had this pillowcase on my pillow ever since I moved from a crib to a bed. It has carried me through numerous nightmares, sleepless nights, and sick days out of school, as well as a move to a new house, slumber parties, and even college! (Yes, college!) People definitely had things to say about an eighteen-year-old with a Snoopy pillowcase, but I didn't care. It was my "security pillowcase," and it made me feel at home wherever I went.

After college, I moved into my own apartment; the pillowcase came with me. I soon met my future husband, who immediately noticed my love for Snoopy. My small apartment was flooded with Snoopy plates, figures, and stuffed Snoopys that I had acquired through the years. I held off showing him the pillowcase, though—I didn't want to scare him away!

As I got to know him better, he began sharing how he also had loved Snoopy while growing up; he remembered owning the Snoopy Scooter Shooter and Snoopy sheets. (We may have had a complete bedding set together!) He always looked forward to *It's the Great Pumpkin, Charlie Brown* and *A Charlie Brown Christmas* every year. I knew he was the one for me: He'd draw me pictures of Snoopy's head, and he gave me a big peanut with Snoopy reclining on top of it.

And he asked me to marry him even *after* he saw the pillowcase!

The pillowcase followed me to our first home, when after a few months I feared that a few more washes would cause it to disintegrate entirely. I sadly folded it up and securely stored it in the basement, where I sometimes go down and look at it and remember the times when it provided comfort for me at night.

Even though Snoopy no longer covers my pillow, he lives with me all over the house: on plates, in snow globes, and on my Snoopy Christmas tree. I'm also known in my neighborhood for my love of Snoopy, thanks to a weather vane on top of the garage—made specially for me—of Snoopy and Woodstock.

Snoopy brought a lot of fun into my life when I was young, and he continues to do so today. I smile when looking at old pictures of me, dressed up like Snoopy for Halloween, or when I take in my ever-growing collection.

But the greatest feeling I get comes when I snuggle up in front of the TV with my husband, while the snow is coming down outside, and we once again hear that familiar music: "Christmastime is here . . ."

Jennifer Ann Schachner

When I was five years old, my parents announced that we were moving from our little house in Brooklyn, New York, to someplace called California. We were to drive there; needless to say, it was a daunting adventure for anyone, no less a small child. Luckily for me, I had a friend named Snoopy, and I knew he'd be with me every step of the way. After all, he had been with me since I was born, and I was sure he had no plans of leaving me now. He surely knew I needed him to tackle this big, scary adventure. I knew his big eyes and red sweatshirt would be with me during this trip, and knowing that made it so much easier.

I could do anything with Snoopy by my side.

The day of packing was a whirlwind of chaos; my parents' friends were literally throwing things in boxes. I was fine as long as Snoopy was in my sight. But suddenly, I turned around and he was gone . . . vanished into thin air. Where did he go?! I needed him to go to California! We couldn't leave him behind!

I began to panic and scream for him, when my mother realized he had been thrown into one of the boxes and was somewhere on the moving truck. All packing stopped, and the search for Snoopy began. Some hours later, he was found upside down in a box with eight-track tapes and clothes hangers. How rude, to place Snoopy in such horrible conditions! Just as Linus's blue security blanket never left his side, Snoopy wasn't supposed to be out of my reach. I needed him to survive, especially since we were going so far!

In every memory I have of that car trip across this country, Snoopy plays a huge part. He was not a stuffed animal, and no one better have called him that. He was *Snoopy*; he had a name and feelings, and I would protect him as he sat next to me in the car. He became my pillow, my blanket, and my best friend. When I was scared of the rain,

I held him tight and he reassured me. When I was tired, he held my head; when I felt lost in another hotel, I always knew I was protected with him around

A few times, I didn't treat Snoopy very well. I was prone to car sickness; unfortunately, Snoopy became the target during some of those episodes. At times, he was dropped on his head, stuffed into a backpack, or kicked off the bed when I moved too quickly in my sleep. He never complained and always forgave me. After all, he was my best friend.

I had to share my best friend once with another old friend: my first dog. They were about the same size, and I think it was love at

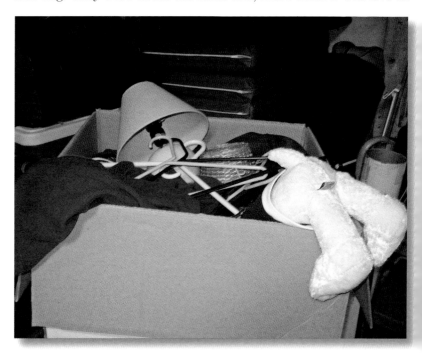

first sight for both of them. We became a group of three, and we were inseparable.

When my family moved across the country to California so many years ago, I had no idea that we were really bringing Snoopy home. Thanks to the Charles M. Schulz Museum, I was recently thrilled to learn more about my best friend and the man who created him.

Snoopy has sat faithfully on my dresser for the past thirty-one years. Every time I pass him, I'm filled with precious memories and feelings.

Thomas G. Storey

I was a pilot in the U.S. Air Force, flying fighter aircraft during the Vietnam War. Our squadron flew F-4s out of Udorn Air Base, in Thailand.

We arrived in-country in October 1966. Most of our missions were flown against targets in North Vietnam. I was shot down just south of the Chinese border on January 16, 1967.

I evaded capture for a week in the heavy mountainous terrain of North Vietnam. I was tracked by dogs and during the ensuing chase was shot by my captors. I then became a prisoner of war.

For 2,240 days.

I was held in the old French prison in downtown Hanoi, which we prisoners named the Hanoi Hilton. After many months of isolation and torture, I joined another American. The two of us lived in a four-by-eight-foot cell for the next three years. The two of us then joined two other Americans, and we were moved to another prison camp, west of Hanoi, near a small Vietnamese village called Son Tay. We named this prison Camp Hope.

None of us, up to this time, had received any correspondence from our families. After four years of captivity, just about Christmastime, I was taken to an interrogation room and was allowed to read my first piece of mail from my family.

The item, a Hallmark *Peanuts* card that featured Snoopy, contained a note and a photograph of my wife and two children. You cannot imagine how that card—of Snoopy and my family—brightened my dreary existence. The interrogator wouldn't let me keep the card or the photograph, but I shall never forget that day.

During my release in March 1973, my captors returned the Snoopy card, along with many letters that had been withheld during my captivity.

From left, Thomas G. Storey, Japanese Hallmark Representative Mr. Suzuki, William Anderson, and a *very* special card

Years later, while serving at Yokota Air Base, Japan, as the commander of the Army and Air Force Exchange Service, I met Bill Anderson. Bill was the Far East sales director for Hallmark International. We sold the Hallmark line of greeting cards in our military stores in Japan. I told him my Snoopy card story.

Several months later, on November 29, 1984, during another visit from Bill, he presented me with a giant Snoopy card signed by Charles M. Schulz. To say that I was surprised would be a tremendous understatement. I shared my delight in a letter to Mr. Schulz, which I wrote on December 6:

Words cannot express my joy and surprise when Bill Anderson from Hallmark International arrived in my office at Yokota Air Base, Japan, on 29 November 1984 and presented to me a Snoopy card with your signature. WOW!

Snoopy has become, over the years, a part of our family. We have used him as our expression of love to each other on birthdays, anniversaries, and Christmases, and any other reason we can think of to exchange cards.

As you know, he even arrived in Hanoi, North Vietnam, during Christmas 1971 and was the first piece of correspondence I received from my family after four years in captivity as a prisoner of war.

By the way, I still have that card.

Snoopy is very popular here in Japan, and you can see his antics everywhere. My wife and I have found several articles of Snoopy clothing to send our grandson for Christmas. Our daughter has decorated his room with nothing but—you guessed it—Snoopy. He even has a Snoopy blanket on his bed and a big stuffed Snoopy, bigger than he is, sitting in the corner. Snoopy is now part of four generations of the Storey family, as my dad, eighty-six years young, also receives Snoopy cards periodically. Snoopy also visits my office every day in the comics section of the Pacific Stars and Stripes newspaper.

This has been the long way around to tell you, sir, just how much your gesture of kindness and thoughtful expression has meant to me. Snoopy is presently being

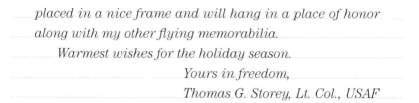

placed in a nice frame and will hang in a place of honor
along with my other flying memorabilia.
Warmest wishes for the holiday season.
Yours in freedom,
Thomas G. Storey, Lt. Col., USAF

I remained in Japan until my retirement from the U.S. Air Force. In 1986, about the time of my retirement, I received a package from Mr. Schulz. It was a twelve-by-twenty-eight-inch framed and signed four-panel comic strip of Snoopy flying his doghouse behind enemy lines. Suddenly he turns his plane around, because something is calling him back:

Doughnuts in the Red Cross tent.

Needless to say, it has a place of honor on the wall in my den.

Mike Burns

In the fall of 1968, as a third-grade schoolboy, I spent several days at an allergy clinic, much of that time in the waiting room. While there, I read children's books the clinic provided: compilations of daily *Peanuts* strips that covered several years from the late 1960s. The first I read was titled *The Unsinkable Charlie Brown*.

After a couple of those, I was hooked. I eventually got Mom to buy me all the *Peanuts* books that were available. In the middle of this mania, one day my Dad asked a disturbing, annoying question: "Why do you read *Peanuts* books so much, Michael? You don't learn anything from 'em." I had no answer. But I didn't forget the question.

A couple of years passed. I read more strips in paperback collections. I read a couple of hardback collections of some of these same strips: *Peanuts Classics* and *The Peanuts Treasury* (with the Sunday strips in color!). Saw the movie *A Boy Named Charlie Brown*; read the book adaptation. Watched the TV specials. It was *so* much fun, even when the question returned: Why did I like *Peanuts* so much?

Adolescence. I grew bored with my old *Peanuts* books and gradually surrendered them to my nephews. They'd usually take them to bed and read themselves to sleep when they stayed at our house. One by one, they took most of the books home with them.

Even so, as high school and college flew by, I still read the current daily and Sunday strips, and my heart would jump with joy at seeing each new one. But why? I didn't "learn anything from 'em."

Then, finally, I was down to one book—*Sunday's Fun Day, Charlie Brown*—and I gave it to my daughter. We'd sit and read the strips together. Like the one where Charlie Brown is ready to trade his whole baseball card collection to Lucy in exchange for a card of Joe Shlabotnik (Charlie Brown's bumbling hero). Lucy, being Lucy, refuses; saddened, Charlie leaves. Lucy tosses the coveted card in the trash. We felt so sorry for Charlie Brown!

The question came back. The answer felt close.

A year later, I saw a magnificent painting of Charlie Brown and Snoopy, looking into each other's eyes. The painting's warm colors, the use of "soft focus," the soulful expressions on these two dear, familiar faces . . . it was like something out of comic-strip heaven. It wasn't Charles Schulz's work, but the painter obviously was an old fan: a kindred soul of Schulz's (and mine) if I ever saw one.

Mike and his daughter, Emaleth, haggle over a baseball card trade

Something clicked. I had an answer now. Why do I read *Peanuts* comic strips? I "don't learn anything from 'em." No, not true. I did—*do*—learn something from 'em.

I learned what kind of soul Schulz had. You can learn that from any artist if you study his work long enough.

And Schulz's soul was beautiful. He enjoyed life so much and wanted so badly for all of us to do the same, and Charlie Brown was the type of person he loved best of all: the plodding, unsung saint who never quits, and whose heart never goes bad . . . a heart that expects life's (and people's) best and believes in that best even when it doesn't appear.

A heart that will always push Charlie Brown to fly another kite, pitch another game, keep loving that little red-haired girl, have another go at kicking Lucy's football, or set yet another good example for a cynical little sister.

Happiness is . . .
Sharing your story!

But, wait . . . the story isn't over yet!

Or, more precisely, more stories are waiting to be shared!

Do you have a favorite *Peanuts*-themed memory? A sweet, amusing, or poignant family anecdote? If so, tell us all about it!

The narrative must be written in the first person ("I've loved *Peanuts* since . . ."), and it must concern a truly pivotal event in your relationship with the *Peanuts* gang. We don't simply want a list of your enormous collection or a short saga about how you adopted a beagle and named it Snoopy. We're after events and encounters that transformed you and/or loved ones: a story that shares how Charlie Brown and his friends became an integral part of your life.

You've just finished a book that is filled with the sort of anecdotes we're after; if you think you can make us laugh or cry just as much as these stories did, then we want to hear from you. Don't worry that your tale might be the same as somebody else's; each person's "take" is always unique.

If we use your story, you'll receive an acknowledgment and a copy of the sequel to this book.

As you can see from the stories published within these pages, we'll also want a photograph to accompany your story: a picture that shows you holding the plush Snoopy you've owned since childhood or standing alongside the handcrafted outdoor *Peanuts* Christmas decoration that has made you a neighborhood icon. Please, though, ask us for photo details when responding with your *Peanuts* anecdote; do *not* send any pictures without first having a chat with us about subject, content, and other issues.

Stories must be accompanied by your mailing address and phone number. Send all submissions by regular mail or e-mail to

Derrick Bang
4350 Cowell Blvd.
Davis, California 95618
(530) 758-9479
Derrick@PeanutsStories.com

We look forward to hearing from you!

About the Authors

Derrick Bang sharpened his reading skills at a young age by paging carefully through the paperback collections of *Peanuts* strips that his father brought as gifts when he returned home from business trips. As Derrick grew older, he enjoyed the daily newspaper dose of *Peanuts*; his fondness for Charles M. Schulz's work eventually built to the sort of passionate dedication that fuels lifelong pursuits. Derrick channeled this devotion into something of a second career: Although a newspaper editor/writer by day, he found time to author two informative and historical books about Schulz's work (*50 Years of Happiness* and *Charles M. Schulz: Li'l Beginnings*) and edit a third (*It's Only a Game*). He hopes *Security Blankets* is merely the next in an ongoing line of *Peanuts*-themed books.

Don Fraser became a fan of *Peanuts* as a U.S. Marine fighter pilot in the late 1950s. He went on to found two international companies, Aviva Enterprises and Inetics, Inc., that created and marketed *Peanuts* character merchandise worldwide. Don was a friend and tennis partner of Sparky Schulz for over thirty-five years. He lives in northern California with his wife, Dianne. They have six children and seven grandchildren.